Jack &

Always be of

Joy Hira

II Cor 12:9

The Holy Spirit Makes

No Earthly Sense

by Terry Rush

INTRODUCTION BY CLINE R. PADEN

HOWARD BOOK HOUSE
107 Yellowood Drive
West Monroe, LA 71291

The Holy Spirit Makes

No Earthly Sense

by Terry Rush

INTRODUCTION

Someone has well said that the most difficult subject to speak on is one that is most often used. The degree of difficulty encountered is determined by the amount of controversy that swirls around the topic being discussed. When a disputable matter is introduced the mind of the auditor often rushes ahead of the speaker to take up his defensive positions which he fears may be assailed. And there he waits until the speaker comes to where he is. If the speaker approaches the holy soil of his prejudices threateningly, he either turns him off completely, or is so busy trying to shore up his preconceived ideas that he does not hear what is said. Writers of debatable themes have the same problem. They can only plead for an unbiased perusal of their material.

Much that is taught today concerning the Holy Spirit is without scriptural warrant. Until recently it was a theme rarely treated in sermon among us. Still fewer have dared to write on the subject. Thus the field has been too long abandoned to the religious fanatic who has taught cunningly devised fables which must have grieved the Holy Spirit of God.

Even the diligent seeker of truth who dares to read this book with his defenses down will find some expressions, phrases, or even concepts with which he cannot agree; but few will be the critics who will remain unchanged.

The writer has plowed some new ground, and the refreshing smell of newly turned soil is invigorating. He has clothed his thoughts in colorful language which enhances the force of his convincing arguments.

Some books are read once and summarily forgotten. I predict that this one will be read and re-read with lingering profit.

Cline R. Paden
Lubbock, Texas

ACKNOWLEDGEMENTS

This material is completed due to a giving crew of motivators and advisers. So many times I wanted to quit.

My Sunday morning students so changed that I could not quit. They became so new. I had to introduce this material.

Shirley English, Barbara Gardner, Rita Risley, Sherri Storm and Velda Watson labored tirelessly over the typewriters and word processors. Too, Linda Jones aided me with the grammatical apsects of the manuscript.

Cline Paden, Richard Baggett and especially Ted Stewart of the Sunset School of Preaching gave suggestions to improve the phrasing of the manuscript.

Finally, thanks to Chris Jones accepting my intrusion one early morning and meeting with me at Arby's. His counsel on that occasion revived me from discouragement and, thus the book did reach completion.

These people offered quality assistance and encouragement to keep going. My heartfelt appreciation is expressed to each for standing with me in this important labor.

Terry Rush

PREFACE

A span of eight years included three feeble attempts on my part to teach a Bible class on the topic of the Holy Spirit. Each effort only proved to increase the already abundant confusion about Him. How could a theme so central to the Christian religion be so elusive? Why did we conclude each series seemingly without progress? We even viewed Him as an "It".

And then the day dawned and the morning star arose and at last . . . . I knew the problem and the cure! Each approach was immediately drawn to wonders and signs. We could never succeed in getting past the stigmas of miracles and tongue-speaking. We were blocked out from discovering just exactly what it is the Holy Spirit does in our lives because we gathered to prove what He was not to do in the lives of others.

As a result, we have a great many hungry and empty students raising the curious question in secrecy: "If the Holy Spirit is dwelling within the believer, what does He do?" If we are to broaden our understanding of God and His real kingdom, we must answer this question.

This book is written to encourage one point: Jesus demonstrates in at least eight steps exactly how the Spirit works in us. He walked to show us how a human being is to make contact with the Spirit from above. He demonstrated how we are to correlate human inadequacy with God power. He literally conveyed this idea: "You have read how fleshly people and God's Spirit were to function together. Now, watch me act it out. Once you have seen me walk in your sandles, you'll see how the Father anticipates that you will walk in His Spirit."

The Word became flesh. We have spoiled that dramatic truth. We have excused ourselves from pure commitment to our Lord by professing that Jesus only did all the great things he did because he was super-human. The role of less life, less service and less conviction is made easy when we perceive Jesus as untouchable.

To the contrary, one's hope is weighty once it is realized Jesus was common . . . man. His birth was not until Mary went full-term. God could as easily sprung him into the flesh a grown man. He was born in a less than common barn. The city is only significant because he was born there.

His disciples were quite average. Their style was not exactly what one could classify as elite. I picture them, at times, on the order of Bob Newhart's Larry and his brother, Daryl, and other brother, Daryl!

Although divine, he so submitted to full-fledged humanity that he did not get all of the breaks in life. So normal was Jesus that he was disliked, betrayed, mocked, trapped, arrested, shamed, advised, overlooked . . . all traits of a person. He was not plastic, mystical nor the exception to the rule.

He had earthly references toward him like son, brother, friend, Joshua, carpenter, teacher and master.

If he was Clark Kent-in-the-flesh why were soldiers able to arrest him? Why did the prison walls stay in tact? Why did the spikes hold? Why did the spear pierce? Why did blood flow? Why did death claim?

The Holy Spirit was the energetic difference in this divine-in-flesh-one. The Spirit shifted Jesus into the pattern of power. His steps were not in size 25 shoe! They were in 1½, 7, 5½, 9D, 4, and 14BB . . . those of people.

His display of the Above dwelling in Beneath was not to corner us into fear and doubt that we could never succeed in Kingdom service. Quite the opposite is true, my friend. The Son of Man pursued, trod and spoke that we might get the picture of the Holy Spirit working within the flesh-person. Even his flesh and blood entered not the territory of Heaven. Even his body was transformed.

Reverence and awe is to be offered more than ever when one catches a glimpse of how humbling it must have been for one who pre-existed in an all-capacity style to be reduced to baby-body, baby-brain, baby-dependence. Joy to the world . . . a Savior was born a person who identifies with disappointment, testing and boondocks.

I have written two books previous to this manuscript. They were easy by comparison. I wrote those two; but have given birth to this one. Trying to express each sentence with precision that would be palatable by every view in our religious body is more than a quest. How do you convey something you fully believe is new and yet clothe it in words and phrases that are old? The labor pains have been fierce.

You may not agree with all that is written. I only ask you to study. This is not the Alpha nor the Omega of Holy Spirit facts. It is aggressive in leading one to capture the fragrance of the Spirit by obtaining a more accurate picture of our brother . . . Jesus.

Students of this material must understand the enormous hesitation I have in putting this in print. It is risky because of those wolves in sheep's clothing who own printing presses. Yet I must risk.

If we do not grow to the practical day-to-day living by the Spirit, we will remain dead while we live. Without Him our religious exercises will only prove more numbing; more deadening. Too, we will drive our own people, especially our teens to drugs, alcohol or even to Spirit error if we do not fill our tabernacles with that for which they crave to be filled . . . the Holy God in Spirit form.

May we take the command to be filled with the Holy Spirit quite seriously. Let not our soberness be found due to lack of wine only, but presence of Spirit (Ephesians 5:18).

Terry Rush
747 South Memorial
Tulsa, Oklahoma 74112

Table Of Contents

CHAPTER 1

THE PARALLEL DESIGN

Holy Offspring

From the beginning of such an exhilarating and yet deep topic, one can be able to better understand the Spirit if we watch Jesus. Look for those subtle maneuvers that are for our learning. Everything he did was to help us. We will approach the study from the parallel concept of birth and the Holy Spirit.

First, the Spirit was involved in the birth of Jesus. To the virgin Mary the angel said, "The Holy Spirit will come upon you and the power of the Most High will overshadow you: and for that reason the holy offspring shall be called the Son of God (Lk. 1:35)." Let us focus upon the involvement of birth in order that it be true to us . . . holy offspring.

One will truly grow toward the Spirit if he can relate to His purpose. In Genesis 1:2, "And the earth was formless and void, and darkness was over the surface of the waters." His work in the following verses was to bring about order and reason and direction. Once all was set into proper formation the earth was able to be fruitful. Everything was in sync.

In the beginning then, the work of the Spirit was to create. In the New Testament era His work is to re-create. Man was created (Gen. 1:26) in Their image, according to Their likeness. Man was like God or God-like. As sin rudely imposed itself upon

13

mankind we all lost our glory of being in Their image (Rom. 3:23). And now we are no longer like God.

Due to His love coupled with unending persistence, He sent His Spirit to re-create that image we once had. Don't hurry past this beautiful reaching heart of the Father. He loves us so much. He saw we were in a sin-bind. We were stranded up to our spiritual necks in debt. We were held hostage by an ugly captor. He sent Jesus to the rescue; himself being the ransom. The cross was only the halfway house for us. We were now debt-free but not restored to Their image.

The Father then sent His Spirit that we might be born -- one more time -- in Their image and the whole nine yards. The difference with this re-creation over the first creation of us? It comes with a written guarantee? "In Him, you also, after listening to the message of truth, the gospel of your salvation - having also believed, you were sealed in Him with the Holy Spirit of promise, who is given as a pledge of our inheritance, with a view to the redemption of God's own possession, to the praise of His glory (Eph. 1:13, 14)."

As He was wonderfully involved in the birth of Jesus, He is in ours. "I say to you, unless one is born again, he cannot see the kingdom of God (Jn.3:3)." Why? Why must we be born again? Because we are no longer like Him. Our first birth was tarnished. The creation of His image "didn't take" just as some of us receive our flu shots and they didn't work right. So, "unless one is born of the water and the Spirit, he cannot enter the kingdom of God (Jn. 3:5)."

What does the Holy Spirit do in this rebirth;

this being born one more time? The same thing He did in His work of the first creation. He now hovers over the deep of people. He takes our emptiness and our chaos and our listless meandering from day to day and year to year and re-creates order, organization, purpose and reason. For what? That our new life can be restored to one of fruitful and powerful expression. He causes life to make sense. Living begins to fit. Our days are filled with aim and direction.

"He saved us, not on the basis of deeds which we have done in righteousness, but according to His mercy, by the washing of regeneration and renewing by the Holy Spirit (Titus 3:5)." "Re-generated" indicates what? We were once generated and needed to have it done over. "Re-newing"? Once new but now the theme is to be new again. How? By the Holy Spirit's activity. So just what is it He does? One of the things is that He "re-starts" us through the processes of life.

Noting the "like-God" emphasis being restored at the "born again" event by the Spirit, watch the words of Romans 6 become so reasonable. "Do you not know that all of us who have been baptized into Christ Jesus have been baptized into His death?" Friend, pause here just a moment. Why meet Him at death? What's the significance? It makes no earthly sense; that's for sure! Look, Jesus lived to show us that our fleshly content had to come to an end. One cannot enter the kingdom by "man-power." He lived teaching us the physical is full of flaws. "Be born one more time," He would say, "and this time make it a spiritual (Spirit) birth."

Continuing in Romans 6, "Therefore we have been buried with Him through baptism into death in order that as Christ was raised from the dead through the glory of the Father, so we too might walk in NEWNESS of life." Now, friend, watch this. "For, IF we have become united with Him in the LIKENESS of His death, certainly, we shall be also in the LIKENESS of His resurrection, knowing this, that our OLD SELF was crucified with Him . . . " Why kill the old self and bury it? Because it is that part of the first birth that was ruined as it was stormed by sin.

Burial is significant. It is more than doctrine. It is wonderful. It's our signal to Him that we are starting again; bringing our old nature to a final halt. We refuse to be a "patchwork" Christian. We want to do totally away with the old unlikeness in order that we can be brand new ---- likeness restored.

The apostle Paul said with great precision, "Therefore from now on we recognize no man according to the flesh; even though we have known Christ according to the flesh, Yet now we know Him thus no longer. Therefore if any man is in Christ, he is a NEW CREATURE: the OLD THINGS PASSED AWAY; behold, new things have come (II Cor. 5:16, 17)." Four marvelous and sensible moves are made in this Corinthian letter:

1. From now on: meaning something is different now. Something has changed. A new development is on the scene.
2. According to the flesh: The new development is that a person can appear outwardly the same after baptism, but it is the inner person that will never be the same again.

Crucified and yet living? Yes, when it is the inner man that is buried. "I have been crucified with Christ; and it is no longer I who lives, but Christ lives in me and the life WHICH I NOW LIVE in the flesh I LIVE BY FAITH in the Son of God, who loves me, and delivered Himself up for me (Gal. 2:20)."

I don't live and yet I do live! Earthly sense? The body is the same. Yet due to the riddance of the old inadequacies, inferiorities and fears, the same body is hardly recognizable. It has within itself new esteem, new confidence, new adequacies. "And such CONFIDENCE we have through Christ toward God. Not that we are adequate in ourselves to consider anything as coming from ourselves, but our adequacy is FROM GOD, who made us adequate as servants of the new covenant, not of the letter, BUT OF THE SPIRIT: for the letter kills, BUT THE SPIRIT GIVES LIFE (II Cor. 3:4-6)."

Born again, there is now a life in which some conditions have drastically changed. Observers can hardly believe (recognize according to the flesh) their eyes. One who has been a nervous wreck is now able to relax. The harsh one is now becoming more gentle. The one out of control is now disciplined. How? Why? Such a one buried the inadequate self -- literally underwent a spirit-transplant. Now he operates on God's Spirit.

17

3. A new creature: Here my friend is a remarkable phenomena. If a way could be devised in which one who is depressed could commit suicide and still be alive afterwards, do you think society would be interested? Most definitely. Friend, this is exactly what we are discussing. We don't care for the way we are? God isn't all that thrilled about it either.

   Through His love he provides a way to bring your misery and your failure to an end. His Spirit will re-create you. You can effectively become a new person. Who wouldn't want to start over if they could? To put all of our "mess-ups", our "hurts" and our "anguishes" in the past only to live from a fresh, debt-free life would be too good to be true! It is true! And, it is why I believe that the gospel is more than "good news". It is "too good of news to be true". Yet is is!

4. Passed away: When your neighbor passes away what do you attend? His funeral. Why? He died. The Spirit moved in at our burial. We are to attend our own funeral. Bury that miserable being and receive new life. Die. Be raised from that grave of water at baptism to live. Live how? In the "likeness" of God. Recreated, renewed, reborn -- a brand new life and a fresh start and greater hope for success . . . it is yours for the believing.
   At this point reread Romans 6:3-6 and II Corinthians 5:16-17.

"Or do you not know that all of us who have been baptized into Christ Jesus have been baptized into His death? Therefore we have been buried with Him through baptism into death, in order that as Christ was raised from the dead through the glory of the Father, so we too might walk in newness of life."

"For if we have become united with Him in the likeness of His death, certainly we shall be also in the likeness of His resurrection, knowing this, that our old self was crucified with Him, that our body of sin might be done away with, that we should no longer be slaves to sin . . . "

And then, "Therefore from now on we recognize no man according to the flesh; even though we have known Christ according to the flesh, yet now we know Him thus no longer. Therefore if any man is in Christ, he is a new creature; the old things passed away; behold new things have come." Let the connection of inner death, burial and restored likeness lead you to Titus 3:4-6.

"But when the kindness of God our Savior and His love for mankind appeared, He saved us not on the basis of deeds which we have done in righteousness, but according to His mercy, by the washing of regeneration and renewing by the Holy Spirit, whom He poured out upon us richly through Jesus Christ our Savior . . . . "

All of this is so simple. Why didn't we know this before? We never read it this way before or we would have believed it years ago.

Hopeful Offspring

A graphic illustration of faith is disclosed in Romans, chapter four: " ... even God, who gives life to the dead and calls into being that which does not exist (v. 17)." Faith is to be involved in the pursuit of regeneration and renewal. We are diligently laboring in the invisible realm. Yet it is very legitimate. Inferiority, depression, doubt, etc., are all of the invisible inner nature — very real.

A possible response to this principle of good news thus far in the first chapter may be "how" does God do this? It sounds good but makes no earthly sense. Dealing with the Creator will always leave us at one place; that of faith. In Romans 4 Abraham is brought up as an ancient demonstrator of what we are to be.

Abraham had been promised by God that he and Sarah would have a child of their own. Years advanced. By fleshly standards and abilities the old couple was fully aware they could not possibly have a baby ... unless God was able to call into being an ability that at this point in their lives frankly did not exist. "In hope against hope he believed, in order that he might become a father of many nations, according to that which had been spoken. So shall your descendants be. And WITHOUT BECOMING WEAK IN FAITH he contemplated his own body as good as dead since he was a hundred years old, and the deadness of Sarah's womb; yet WITH RESPECT TO THE PROMISE OF GOD, HE DID NOT WAVER in unbelief, but grew strong in faith, giving glory to God, and being fully

20

ASSURED THAT WHAT HE HAD PROMISED, HE WAS ABLE ALSO TO PERFORM (Rom. 4:18-21)."

Can you become new? Can a new personality develop from within? If it were to happen to you would it be almost impossible to believe? Would it be like calling something into existence out of nothing? Listen to me now, God wants to go to work recreating you from the inside. He has conveyed a promise. "If you will believe then be buried and I'll be there to remodel you from the inside by the working of My Spirit." "For the promise is for you and for your children, and for all who are far off, as many as the Lord our God shall call to Himself (Acts 2:39)."

As you ponder this venture keep in mind that He has promised. God is ready and willing to gut out your earthly habitation and so remodel that the fragrance of this new interior will be sweet and wonderful "For we are a fragrance of Christ . . . (II Cor. 2:15)." He specializes in buying up weary, worn and run down lives. He loves it. He loves to create new people within themselves as much as some of you love to do crafts or go fishing. God is a very practical Father. It's just that His interests make no earthly sense. Therefore, His first love becomes a mighty challenge to our feeble-by-comparison minds. So, we are called upon to believe it possible. Our responsibility is to "walk by faith and not by sight (II Cor. 5:7)." Just as one would enter surgery due to a faulty heart for the transplant of a healthy one, we are to yield by faith to the Spirit transplant.

Consider these "first-birth" "first creation" passages:

21

1. "Let Us make man in our image, according to Our Likeness . . . (Gen. 1:26)."
2. "And the Lord God fashioned into a woman the rib which He had taken from the man, and brought her to the man (Gen. 2:22)." (Friend, if God can create man out of dust and woman out of a rib He can certainly recreate happiness, peace and hope out of paranoia, sorrow and perplexity.)
3. "The Spirit of God has made me, and the breath of the Almighty gives me life . . .
   . . . Behold, I belong to God like you; I too have been formed out of clay (Job. 33:4, 6)."

Of course John 3:3-5, Romans 6:3-6, II Corinthians 5:16, 17 and Titus 3:5 have been discussed thus far in connecting the Holy Spirit's involvement in the "second-birth". Add these two:

1. "Then the Spirit of the Lord will come upon you mightily, and you shall prophesy with them and BE CHANGED INTO ANOTHER MAN (I Sam. 10:6)."
2. "Blessed be the God and Father of our Lord Jesus Christ, who according to his great mercy has caused us to be born AGAIN TO A LIVING HOPE through the resurrection of Jesus Christ from the dead . . . (I Pet. 1:3)."

The Holy Spirit's activity can be understood. You are well on your way to an exciting adventure as we continue to unfold truth of the Spirit with incredible simplicity. The Holy Spirit makes no earthly sense. But He surely does make heavenly sense on the inside. Now that, my friend, is good stuff!

Wholly Offspring

At the event of the "Word becomes flesh" being baptized, a major bulletin was issued. The message has filled the air waves ever since. ". . . and a voice came out of heaven, 'Thou art My beloved Son, in Thee I am well-pleased (Lk. 3:22).'" Jesus, the fleshly one, is announced to be the Holy Father's child. The marvelous parallel continues of "so goes Jesus, so goes us". And the same is spoken of us.

"For YOU ARE SONS OF GOD through faith in Christ Jesus. For all of you who were baptized into Christ have clothed yourselves with Christ (Gal. 3:26-27)." Sons of God to what extent? To the fullest. God is our Father. He loves, He gives, He disciplines. He loved Jesus and He loves us. He gave strength to Jesus and He gives strength to us. He disciplined Jesus and He disciplines us.

The fact that Jesus needed discipline lets us view him as a little more normal. Maybe he is like us after all. "In the days of his flesh, he offered up both prayers and supplications with loud crying and tears to the One able to save him from death, and he was heard because of His piety. ALTHOUGH HE WAS A SON, HE LEARNED OBEDIENCE from the things which he suffered. And having BEEN MADE perfect, He became to all those who obey Him the source of eternal salvation. . . (Heb. 5:7-9)."

Jesus led the way in the "flesh walk by Spirit trends". He was God's Son. He pioneered the way for others to be adopted into the Holy Family. We are no less His real children. He places us in the family will. We will be receiving an inheritance as brothers and sisters of Christ. "And if you belong to Christ, then you are Abraham's offspring, and heirs

23

according to promise (Gal. 3:29)."

You are Abraham's offspring. Guess who else is. Jesus. "The book of the genealogy of Jesus Christ, the son of David, the son of Abraham (Mt. 1:1)." Luke 3:34 restates and solidifies the truth that Jesus is a direct descendent of Abraham. Scripture says we are, too.

"But if the Spirit of Him who raised Jesus from the dead dwells in you, He who raised Christ Jesus from the dead will also give life to your mortal bodies through His Spirit who indwells you. So then, brethren, we are under obligation, not to the flesh, to live according to the flesh — for if you are living according to the flesh, you must die; but if by the Spirit you are putting to death the deeds of the body, you will live. For all who are being led by the Spirit of God, THESE ARE SONS OF GOD (Rom. 8:11-14)."

These five verses are very important. When Jesus received the Spirit he was openly declared the Son of God. When we are baptized according to Jesus — not according to John — we receive forgiveness of sins and the Holy Spirit (Acts 2:38). If we are led by the Spirit we are His children. I ask this question. "How can we have any hope of being led by the Spirit if we don't know Him; who He is, what He does, or how He goes about it?" It is my observation that without the Holy Spirit the Bible only makes earthly sense.

I am thoroughly persuaded that the scriptures become nothing more than a mere book of "blah" if we are not Spirit led. How is it that so very many who attend church can't make this power-house of a volume work? We are Spiritless. And friend, until

24

we can concede that Jesus was virtually as ordinary as we, Biblical instruction will forever be held captive by earthly sense and earthly wisdom.

Ordinary as we? Does this not demote the diety of Jesus? Does such a statement not reduce him from the glory of the Sovereign One? May God forbid. It enhances his Lofty Stature. God's tender and merciful heart is shown in the dispatching of the Word-to-earth in flesh form.

It is the subtle mistake of viewing Jesus as Clark Kent-in-the-flesh that is gumming the Kingdom's cylinders. He was sent to be LIKE us — Heb. 2:14, 17. He took on the form of a bond-servant made in the LIKENESS of men — Phil. 2:7.

Did he have the ability to be different than us? Better than us? Above us? Yes. Yet he chose to maintain the posture of a common man. Look at his birth, his home, his location, his appearance and even his selection of the twelve. Every instance — every one — has one overwhelming trademark. . . plain.

If this is not true, why become flesh? Why not become a bronze statue? A complex computer? He did not come to save statues nor computers, but persons. Flesh says he was ordinary.

Why is this so strenuous to accept? It seems that we can say the Son was totally God and totally man with unanimous approval. Yet, make the statement that he was a person and gears shift. Such is made to sound as if one just profaned his name.

Was he an ordinary man? He died, didn't he? He so thoroughly identifies with us. He became one of us.

Therefore, we are full-fledged children belonging to His family because we've been adopted. We wear His name proudly. We can say with an assuring smile that He is our Father. "For we have not received a spirit of slavery leading to fear again, but you have received a spirit of adoption as sons by which we cry out 'Abba! Father' (Rom. 8:15)." We know Him personally and intimately as he conveys the family structure of the Kingdom.

"But when the fulness of time came, God sent forth His Son, born of a woman, born under the Law, in order the He might redeem those who are under the Law, THAT WE MIGHT RECEIVE THE ADOPTION AS SONS. And because you are sons, GOD HAS SENT FORTH THE SPIRIT OF HIS SONS INTO OUR HEARTS, crying 'ABBA FATHER!' Therefore you are no longer a slave, but a son; and if a son then an heir through God (Gal. 4:4-7)." Ordinary people suddenly being considered in the same relationship as Jesus? This can only be possible because of His Spirit functioning within us.

No one has to remain an orphan. Left stranded in life with no heavenly Father is a decision. To remain hopeless is because we choose to stay hopeless. God has spent His Son and His Spirit entirely on us. "And I will ask the Father, and He will give you another Helper, that He may be with you forever, that is the Spirit of truth, whom the world cannot receive, because it does not behold him or know him, but you know him because he abides with you and will be in you. I WILL NOT LEAVE YOU AS ORPHANS: I will come to you (Jn. 14:16-18)." Come to you? Not leave you as orphans?

True. He will return in Spirit to dwell within. Neither will they be hopeless, helpless or homeless. "After a little while the world will behold Me no more; but you will behold me; because I live, you shall live also. In that day you shall know that I am in My Father, and you in Me and I in you (Jn. 14:19, 20)." In you: what form and how? Friend, in God-form by Spirit content. God operated through the invisible nature of real life. One of the tremendous advantages of His locating within us is that we become His children.

It is quite significant, too, that we now discuss another benefit of this Holy indwelling. We can be encouraged that we are involved heavily with the same Spirit Jesus had. We do not receive a "brand B", "sub-par", "semi-effective" spirit. We receive the only Holy One — Eph. 4:4. "There is one body and one Spirit. . . . " "For by one Spirit we are all baptized into one body, whether Jews or Greeks, whether slaves or free, and we were all made to drink of one Spirit (I Cor. 12:13)." We are in tune with the one and only Spirit. The one that empowered Jesus and indwelt Peter empowers and ind-wells God's child today. The access is to the same Spirit.

"For through him we both have our access in one Spirit to the Father (Eph. 2:19)." Let this build a dynamic and energetic confidence from within. We have God-Talent and God-Presence inside of our chipped and cracked earthen vessels. His glory of public recognition is given when society becomes aware that nobodies like us apparently have a nature that is different. And not oddly different but sweetly and attractively so.

The Spirit moved toward the "Word became flesh" and immediately it was declared Jesus is God's Son. We find the same wonder and glory available. The God that walked with Abraham wants to walk with us. The Spirit that lived within Thomas can be living within you.

Sonship is a Bible declared and promoted theme. The lonely person finds a real and spiritual family that loves him. The pauper finds his name included in the will of the Father of all fathers. The nobody finds fellowship with a new family that has become somebody only because of God's adoptive love and compassion.

The church, which is comprised of born-over believers, is real family. It is not a conglomeration of pretense. It is filled with "one-another" style. Encourage one another. Admonish one another. Pray for on another. Build up one another. Motivate one another. Love one another.

Lonely? Not in a crowd of others. Poor? Not in brothers or sisters; family. A nobody? Not when various members of the family need you in their midst and miss you when you are absent.

Friend, earthly sense says life begins at forty. However, real life begins at new birth becoming a child of God. Again, Jesus paved the way. Baptized? Why? To example the process for his potential brothers and sisters — you and me.

May your potential be realized.

CHAPTER 2

THE PARALLEL BAPTISM

Neither the Spirit nor God nor baptism will make any earthly sense. Thinking must be lifted to heights of spirit levels. What we look for must be real. Religion of pretense is worth total rejection. Philosophy of facade is repulsive. We hunger from within for the true; the real. Our success in our probe is determined by where we look.

Where Do We Start?

". . . while we look not at the things which are seen, but at the things which are not seen; for the things which are seen are temporal, but the things which are not seen are eternal (II Cor. 4:18)." Concentration upon invisible areas is what successful life is all about. A Christian is to be deeply involved in a life that is far more exaggerated than the Twilight Zone or Star Wars. Look for yourself. Name the novel that has the mystique of the parting of the Red Sea. What plot is more dramatic than the suspense of Esther? What work has a greater element of surprise than the Resurrection? The God-production is awarded best emotion picture!

We look for the angels to work (Heb. 1:14). We anticipate that the Invisible One will supply all of our needs from above (Phil. 4:19). We expect all things asked in prayer to be received (Mt. 21:22). The student of the Word centers attention on the faith realm. It is sometimes said that a person shouldn't go by blind faith. Well, friend, sight faith doesn't exist. There is no such thing as sight faith. We are to walk by faith, not by sight. Faith casts us into the invisible. We expect, anticipate, hope and believe. Such makes no earthly sense. We are daring to set our eyes upon that which is not obvious to the naked eye. Where do we start? By looking in the direction of the invisible.

"Therefore, (II Cor. 4:16) we do not lose heart, but though our OUTER MAN is decaying, yet our INNER MAN is being RENEWED day by day." Listen to me now. This is it. All is so invisibly clear! The outer man — that exterior flesh — decays through age. Hair grays. Teeth rot. Faces wrinkle. Knees ache. That part of man — outer — that did not die at baptism will eventually fit into its own earthly grave. The part of us — inner — that did die at baptism will never die again. It gets newer every day.

Now friend, let me ask you this. When you attend a funeral, which is present? The outer or the inner person? The outer. That very part that we could see and that we would have verified as the real has ended. Abruptly the visible no longer lasts. Like magic you see it, think its real and then "poof" it's gone.

The inner part is not present at the funeral. The personality, the emotion, the will, the conscience and the mind. . . all are gone. That is the part, though, that continues to live forever. The invisible, it turns out, is the real after all. Drive down the street. Note all of the visible things like trees, cars and buildings. They all look real. Ask yourself this question. How many of these that "are seen" will be around in ten years? One hundred years? One thousand years?

Friend, it is the invisible that is real. Is it wise, then, to live by the law of faith? "Now faith is the assurance of things hoped for, the conviction OF THINGS NOT SEEN. For by it the men of old gained approval. By faith we understand that the worlds were prepared by the Word of God, so that WHAT IS SEEN WAS NOT MADE out of things which are visible (Heb. 11:1-3)."

To look at the eternal invisible (II Cor. 4:18) is merely God's way of being practical. He is directing us to watch for the things that will always last. This certainly makes no earthly sense. But even the earth is heavily threatened to quickly become nonexistent by the potential of nuclear war. Our minds want relief from this fear of "the end". Our system craves for a renewal that will not fade but last forever. Look upon the invisible.

Soil Samples and Lab Tests

As we deepen our probe into the topic of the Holy Spirit, we continue to pick up significant cues from the Son of man. This next trek through scripture will be extremely, as well as extensively, important. Thorough examination of the Word becoming flesh is crucial. I am convinced that the "too good of new to be true" (gospel) is heavily centered upon Jesus moving from His heavenly abode to experience on the job training in the field of human living. He did his practice teaching for thirty-three years. He did soil samples and lab tests clothed in flesh and blood.

"Have this attitude in yourselves which was also in Christ Jesus, who although He existed in the form of God, did not regard equality with God a thing to be grasped, but emptied Himself, taking the form of a bond-servant, and BEING MADE IN THE LIKENESS OF MEN (Phil. 2:5-7)." There's that word again: likeness. Recall we were originally created in His likeness only to watch our resemblance fade. And then He recreated us by calling us to be born over.

This text reveals the interest of God. Knowing full-well we had been created in His image, He saw us slip. The heart of Jehovah is marvelously displayed. He loved us so much that He gave us His Son. The role of Jesus was one: BE LIKE MEN. Be in their likeness. Should He not take on our form, we would be cut off totally and completely from any hope. Slowly ponder this next text of Hebrews 2:14-18:

:14 "Since then the children share in flesh and blood, He Himself likewise also partook of the same, that through death He might render powerless him who had the power of death, that is the devil:. . . " Jesus became flesh and blood — human — that He could prove that even the ultimate power of Satan, which was death of all mankind, would be reduced to shreds.

:15 ". . . and might deliver those who through fear of death were subject to slavery all their lives." No longer are we to be afraid of dying. We have such an invisible concentration that we breeze through the funeral, through the grave and on out the other side of the tomb!

:16 "For assuredly He does not give help to angels, but He gives help to the descendant of Abraham." He does not exist to assist the angelic civilization. And friend, we are no angels! But, he does give help to human beings — people of the family tree of Abraham. Be encouraged. We need help because life is too complex, too unfair, too hopeless for us to handle on our own. He "lived and lives" to give us help.

:17 "Therefore, He had to be made like His brethren in all things, that He might become a merciful and faithful high priest in things pertaining to God, to make propitiation for the sins of the people." HAD TO BE MADE LIKE us. Why? That He could be merciful — understanding and sympathetic toward our weaknesses. "For we do not have a high priest who cannot sympathize with our weaknesses. Let us therefore draw near WITH CONFIDENCE to the throne of grace, that we may receive mercy and may find grace TO HELP IN TIME OF NEED (Heb. 4:15, 16)."

Too, in verse 17 of chapter two, He made propitiation (pro-pish-ia-shun) for the sins of the people. Jesus specialized in curing sinners. He lives to do that! He loves to do that! He wants to do that! Let him do that! We try to get ourselves legally right with God by trying to do enough good things to offset the bad things. It is Jesus — the only Jesus — that can offset our deep sin problem. "My little children, I am writing these things to you that you may not sin. And IF ANYONE SINS, we have an Advocate with the Father, JESUS CHRIST THE RIGHTEOUS; and He Himself is the propitiation FOR OUR SINS; and not for ours only, but also for those of the whole world (I Jn. 2:1, 2)."

He will be such an adequate attorney at the judgement setting because he walked in our sandals. He will attest to the elements of bewilderment, confusion, mistakes, discouragement. He will see that we are covered as he has in his possession the bill sent from Heaven's accounting department showing our sin debt. . . marked "PAID".

:18 "For since He Himself was tempted in that which He has suffered, He is able to come to the aid of those who are tempted." How can he be of any real help? Keep in mind that "real help" is "invisible help". Do realize now that Jesus became human so that he could relate. He experienced fatigue, pressure and disappointment — as a human. He knows what it is LIKE to be you. . . to be me.

Could Jesus Ever Be Unable?

The reason Jesus was baptized was to show us he could do nothing as a person apart from the power of the Father. We mar the beauty of Jesus when we accredit him as doing successful things because he was God. He said, ". . . the Son can do nothing of Himself, unless it is something He sees the Father doing. . . (Jn. 5:19)." He could not do anything of Himself. Why? He was a volunteer human. And, humans can't do anything apart from the invisible. That was his whole reason to become LIKE US in the first place.

It is my conviction that he could do nothing apart from the Father because he was genuinely human. Some may feel that he made this statement on the basis that he and the Father simply could never be separated. One who holds this view may be right. However, the Father and Son did part ways at the cross. They were separable.

Too, verse :18 finds Jesus being accused of being on the same plateau as God. His own words seem — to me — to be assuring those in his presence that such was not the case. "Equality? No, apart from the Father I couldn't do anything."

To ignore this paramount truth is deadening. Until we can believe this, our Christian walk will forever be as the struggle of running a hundred yard dash. . . in sand.

Further documentation that Jesus was all boy is found in a verse earlier discussed. Philippians 2:6, 7 firmly supports that he did not hold on to maintaining his status of being like God. What do you think "emptied" meant? Emptied of what? His being on the level and of the nature of the invisible God. Thus, He took on the form of a servant — plain, normal, common.

Too, I mean no irreverence by insisting that he was plain, ordinary, or all boy. Quite the opposite is intended. Our lack of faith in letting God be all-able is hinged upon the truth that we have yet to let Jesus be all-unable. The Father and the Son were always one: harmonious, but they were not always equal.

Slow down at this curve. Note carefully that I did say they were always one; always harmonious. I did say they were not always equal. That's also what he said through Phil. 2:6, 7... he did not regard equality with God a thing to be maintained.

Such expressions are biblical and have absolutely no cause to fracture the diety of Jesus. He upheld that berth throughout.

To restrict Jesus from becoming totally average via humanity is to treat him as an exchange student. Such leaves him only as an honorary member of our society. The contrary is the truth. He did not visit our planetary system; rather, he fit into it fully. He lived as an earthen one to show us that we can do what he did. A later chapter will devote more attention to this concept.

It is he who even parallels us with himself. He says the same thing about us that he does of himself. "Abide in Me, and I in you. As the branch cannot bear fruit of itself, unless it abides in the vine, so neither can you, unless you abide in Me. I am the vine, you are the branches: he who abides in Me, and I in him, he bears much fruit: FOR APART FROM ME YOU CAN DO NOTHING (Jn. 15:4, 5)." NO THING can be done! He said it of himself. He said it of us. Meaning? The two of us are on equal turf.

I must proceed with caution with this segment as I so deeply desire that one not be lead to a wreckless conclusion. When I say the two of us are on equal turf, such must be conditioned. Equality is in regard to Jesus then (human) and us now. We are not equal in diety. . .we are not diety, although we have the divine nature. We do not carry the qualification that would position us to be worshipped.

It is in the realm of ability; fruit-bearing that John 5:18, 19 and 15:4, 5 are declared. There is no intention, subtle or otherwise, of inferring that we are HOLY AS THOU. These passages make us not the potential objects of worship. They do make us the potential tools of service. Our abilities are awesomely powerful in superlative fashion.

I refuse to give in to letting our people continue to say the right words and yet serve in such a humanistic order. Jesus was able because of God. Could he have done it on his own? If he could, he refused to do so to lead us to dependency. He lived as a dependent human.

Yes, he could have called in 10,000 angels. Yes, he could have done all things differently. BUT HE DIDN'T. He depended on the Father of Power. . .SO MUST WE!

If we are equal to Jesus and nothing can be done by us without Him, then could the same be said about ourselves. . .no one can do anything without us? Keep in mind our equal turf is only in the field of humanity. He could do nothing apart from God because the Father was positioned in the elevated, spirit capacity; Jesus-only human. We can do nothing apart from Jesus WHEN it is he that is in the spirit slot and we — only human.

All of humanity is dependent on Jesus. Such is the key: dependency. He volunteered to be unable resting his work on the Father. We are unable until we rely upon Him.

Since he voluntarily was alone and unable on his own he made a move that revolutionized the Christian age. When Jesus was baptized it has been feebly reasoned that he did it to be a good example. No. No. No. He did it to receive the Holy Spirit. Jesus never did anything powerful nor potent until he was empowered by the eternal, invisible realm. "Now it came about when all the people were baptized, that Jesus also was baptized, and while He was praying, heaven was opened, the Holy Spirit descended upon Him (Lk. 3:21, 22)." He was never the same MAN again. He hit every burg and city with beauty and light and love. He was able and wise and effective.

We are called upon to follow suit. If he, being susceptible to human inadequacies, found invisible ability, he did so to lead the way for us. He set the standard: the pace, the way. So, for us? "Repent and let each of you be baptized in the name of Jesus Christ for the forgiveness of your sins; and YOU SHALL RECEIVE THE GIFT OF THE HOLY SPIRIT (Acts 2:38)." For what? Oh, not much, just a token of his appreciation for being baptized — kind of like receiving a paperweight for donating to the bowling league. Not hardly! Listen to me now. We have avoided this long enough. The Spirit is given to live inside of us in a working way. As He empowered the "Word became flesh," He likewise empowers the "flesh always been flesh!"

Later chapters will deal with the "how". For now we must recognize that Jesus did good and effective works to demonstrate that the Spirit can do the same with us. Jesus never performed a miracle for himself. And due to the Spirit doing "some" wonders we have overlooked the power of enthusiasm and courage, etc. that he provides.

Baptism does for us what it did for Jesus. The Holy Spirit enters our earthen vessel. A new stamina is evident. Baptism for us is tightly knitted to the receiving of the Spirit. As a matter of fact, the Apostle Paul seriously doubted the Ephesian church's accuracy of understanding on this matter. "'Did you receive the Holy Spirit when you believed?' And they said to him, 'No, we have not even heard whether there is a Holy Spirit.' And he said, 'Into what were you baptized?' and they said, 'Into John's baptism.' And Paul said, 'John baptized with the baptism of repentance, telling the people to believe in him who was coming after him, that is, Jesus.' And when they heard this, they were baptized in the name of the Lord Jesus (Acts 19:2-5)." Paul knew that the lack of the Spirit was caused by a misunderstanding of baptism.

John the Baptist baptized for the remission of sins. No Holy Spirit was connected nor involved. Thus Paul's detection was legitimate. The Ephesians had never heard about the Spirit. Friend, many of us still haven't. I question the unending persistence that we be baptized for the remission of our sins. Such is only half accurate. Sins are removed and the Holy Spirit is to move in.

I know of many who heard that they were to be baptized for the forgiveness of their sins, but never heard anything about the Holy Spirit. Without the Holy Spirit one is forever wandering through life making earthly sense. With the Spirit the wandering is transformed into direction and simultaneously it makes no earthly sense. No longer are we backed by Ft. Knox. Suddenly we are backed by the Invisible Eternal Creator. Even Jesus needed to be immersed. We've never let this be so. Jesus was a man on definite target. He was no political showboat. His maneuvers in life were always geared purposely to let us see how to live.

The topic doesn't end here. In chapter three the theme will continue. Let it be noted again that Jesus, the Son of Man, did all that he did to say, "You can do it!" Apart from the Father he could do nothing. With the Father? He could do God's will. Apart from the Spirit of Jesus we can do nothing. With Him? We can do God's will. Thank our gracious Father that Jesus would be so "down-to-earth" and yet operate by that unseen standard that makes no earthly sense.

CHAPTER 3

THE PARALLEL FULNESS

Any reason for substantial hope to be equipped for the task is gained from being filled by the Spirit. Such is a Bible message. Such is intended for modern day disciples. And, such was true of the one who walked the flesh-in-sync-with-Spirit-ways . . .Jesus. He, again, exemplifies that a mortal container can be filled with new spirit content.

Luke 4:1, "And Jesus, full of the Holy Spirit, returned from the Jordon and was led about by the Spirit in the wilderness. . ." Full of the Spirit is that mysterious component that transformed inability to ability and inadequacy to adequacy. It makes no earthly sense. Yet it is full of legitimacy and reason.

Acknowledgement must be given to the fact that the gospel writer felt it significant that the readers understand it was the Holy Spirit that lead the Man. Yes, Jesus may have been able to do all of this on his own spirit ability. Let it be impressivie that this revealed word evidently has a point in this text and others that the diety in man-form was led by the Holy Spirit.

"Jesus returned to Galilee in the power of the Spirit (Lk 4:14)." This is not the unusual, miraculous or fanatical. Spirit power is as necessarily normal for every Christian as is momentum for a winning team. It is not as sensational as it is practical. If Jesus has not the power from on high, then what? He is left to deal with life on his own energy.

Acts 4:31 verifies the church concretely and perpetually moved ahead as followers were filled with the Spirit and began to speak the word with boldness. This supplements our discussion in chapter four of the connection of being equipped for evangelism. These common ones in Acts 4 were not filled to do the weird. They were provided strength to do the necessary.

As the twelve summoned the congregation in Acts 6 they instructed the family of God to select seven men from among them to serve. As one analyzes verse three it makes earthly sense for two of the qualifying conditions: reputable and wise. ABC Brick and Co. would expect the same of their foreman. To be full of the Spirit, though, is not an earthly sense category. Such is a factor only — and I do mean only — in following the Christ.

Examine our preachers. There is no substitute for Spirit within the proclaimer. Notes can be orderly, appearance can be impressive, voice can bellow like ocean waves and yet the message be like cardboard. I think that all preachers have their off days. But many of us are ailing from profound lack of enthusiasm which is only realized when the Spirit of God is within.

Nor do we need to be men of dance, prance, pump and pound. Yet, it remains true that churches are hurting because while truth is being defended it is simultaneously being blasphemed by the form of godly delivery with no power. One cannot have the truth without the Spirit — John 4:24.

Bible class teachers will find themselves ahead in effectiveness if more concentration would be on believing they are filled with the Spirit and less concentration on filling their libraries with the latest innovative materials. The church is at the threshold of unconquerable increase if we can only acknowledge that we are filled with the Holy God in spirit form.

It Begins With The Mind

How? How does one get to that point? When we become open to God's will, we will discover so much of the Word that will fill us with faith. Be transformed by an open and ready to change mind. In so doing, one will prove God's intention (Rom. 12:2).

"For this reason I bow my knees before the Father, from whom every family in heaven and on earth derives its name, that He would grant you according to the riches of His glory, to be strengthened with power through His Spirit in the inner man; . . . (Eph. 3:14-16)."

The ordinary Christian man and woman is sought by the Lord to be given energy empowered from the Most Powerful! Located? In the inner man. The inner — inside man. The part that dies at baptism is the part reborn due to SPIRITUAL rebirth. The inward person consists of mind, emotion, affection, determination, motivation, conscience, etc. (Gal. 3:22, 23 has the Spirit bearing fruit from within the mortal. All of the fruit is an inner characteristic: love (emotion, affection), joy (emotion, affection), peace (mind, emotion, conscience), patience (mind, emotion, motivation, determination), kindness (emotion, affection), goodness (mind, affection, conscience), faithfulness (mind, conscience), gentleness (mind, emotion, affection), self-control (mind, emotion, determination, motivation); against such there is no law.

As one matures in understanding that newly acclaimed power resides actively, new results can be expected. Continue with Eph. 3:17-19. The inner man is given Heavenly strength "so that" (:17):

A. So that Christ may dwell in your hearts (:17). Does this not imply — even insist — that Jesus can't dwell within each of us except by the working of the Spirit?

B. So that we may be able to comprehend with all other believers the entire scope of Christ (:18). Looking for good films, good books, good instructors about the topic of Jesus lately? Look within.

C. So that we can know the love of Christ (:19). It seems consistent that the less one knows of the love of Jesus the more one is legalistic. Spirit and law don't mix.

D. So that you may be filled up to the fulness of God (:19). Me? You mean me? Filled to the capacity of God? Wasn't that just for those like Abraham, Moses, Esther, Mary, Jesus and Peter? No. No. No. We are to be full of God. Full! Full! Full!

Continuing the evaluation of this Ephesian text some revolutionary incite may be gained. Do you or any of your friends ever battle with emptiness? Have you ever considered the solution is Spirit? Empty by depression? An inner problem. Empty by little to teach your class? An inner problem. Empty to face your job each morning? An inner problem. Empty to deal with challenging circumstances? An inner problem. The solution? It begins in Ephesians

3:16 — believe He strengthens.

It is not to be taken lightly the expectation of God that we be like Jesus. Such is His ever driving theme. Eph. 4:13 says we are to so understand the nature of him that we be of the stature which belongs to the fulness of Christ. Quite frankly, we may not have given this serious attention because we don't want to bother to reach that high.

Be encouraged that he reached this low in order that he could show us how to get that high. The only way we can do it is the very way he did it — by being, like-wise, empowered by the Holy Spirit. Jesus was not a mentor of the Spirit. The Spirit was not a tag-along kid brother to Jesus. The only avenue of the Mortal One was the intense activity of the Invisible One. We are to be filled with the Force.

" And do not get drunk with wine, for that is dissipation, but be filled with the Spirit. . . (Eph. 5:18)." Who? Whoever has the potential of getting drunk with wine. We are to be filled not with spirits of this world but with the Spirit of that world. The kingdom of God does not find its citizens filled with earthly dependence but with Spirit supremacy (Rom. 14:17).

Too, note the inner experience of the Christians on the day the church was born. "And everyone kept feeling a sense of awe. . . (Acts 2:43)." Friend, it is always an awesome feeling to witness the children of God alive on earth. Multiples filled with the awesome Spirit cannot maintain any complacent satisfaction with the status quo.

What is the difference in the people of Acts 2:37 compared to the same people and the same setting in verse 43? One thing. They received the Holy

Spirit. They moved from depression, confusion and fear to ultra amazement.

Romans 14:17 calls for intentional and assertive progression to be toward kingdom living and Holy Spirit operation. "The kingdom of God is not eating and drinking, but righteousness and peace and joy IN THE HOLY SPIRIT." Seeing the kingdom any other way is quicksand. Food and drink (the avoidance of nor the indulgence in) will not make me right, at peace, or happy.

A. Righteousness in the Holy Spirit. "He saved us, NOT ON THE BASIS OF DEEDS which we have done in righteousness, but according to His mercy, by the washing of regeneration and renewing BY THE HOLY SPIRIT whom He poured out upon us richly through Jesus Christ our Savior, that being JUSTIFIED BY HIS GRACE we might be made heirs according to the hope of eternal life (Titus3:3-7)."

"For I bear them witness that they have a zeal for God, but not in accordance with knowledge. For NOT KNOWING ABOUT GOD'S RIGHTEOUSNESS, AND SEEKING TO ESTABLISH THEIR OWN, they did not subject themselves to the righteousness of God. For Christ IS THE END OF THE LAW FOR RIGHTEOUSNESS to everyone who believes (Rom. 10:2-4)."

B. Peace in the Holy Spirit. "So the church throughout all Judea and Galilee and Samaria ENJOYED PEACE, being built up; and, going on in the fear of the Lord and in the COMFORT OF THE HOLY SPIRIT, it continued to increase (Acts 9:31)."

"Therefore having been justified by faith, WE HAVE PEACE WITH GOD through our Lord Jesus Christ, through whom also we have obtained our introduction by faith into this grace in which we stand; and we exult in hope of the glory of God. And not only this, but we also exult in our tribulations, knowing that tribulation brings about perseverance; and perseverance proven character; and proven character, hope; and hope does not disappoint, because the love of God has been poured out within our hearts through the HOLY SPIRIT WHO WAS GIVEN TO US (Rom. 5:1-5)."

C. Joy in the Holy Spirit. "And the disciples were CONTINUALLY FILLED WITH JOY AND WITH THE HOLY SPIRIT (Acts 13:52)."

"Now may the God of hope FILL YOU WITH ALL JOY AND PEACE in believing, that you may abound in hope BY THE POWER OF THE HOLY SPIRIT (Rom 15:13)."

"You also became imitators of us and of the Lord, having received the word in much tribulation WITH THE JOY OF THE HOLY SPIRIT. (I Thes. 1:6)."

The righteousness, peace and joy that is from God comes by the Holy Spirit. As various glands produce vital energy to keep the outer body stable, the Spirit produces necessary power to keep the inner person able. False righteousness, false peace and false joy can be interpreted only as momentary and temporary.

False righteousness is based on "scorecard" work. The numbers are there to report - along with the smugness and the arrogance. Read Luke 18:9. A certain one trusted in himself that he was right with God. He had the deeds to prove it. . . to God, no less. Another was so poor in spirit he had nothing to offer as worthy evidence. Himself, his sins, and his hopeful faith was all he had to offer.

God says the latter went home justified. The other one went home damned. Too many workers will be damned because their motivation is self-inflicted self-trust. Faith will always be the work assigned to the follower of Jesus (Jn. 6:29).

False peace is a nightmare. It is a present day holocaust. Peace found in drink and drugs is a nightmare. It is a temporary facade that demands increased repetition. Even apart from alcohol and pills the law abiding member of the church is deceived. He or she can find themselves so at peace (?) with the Lord that they are a nervous wreck about the future of the church. Such irony!

Some have left the church due to impatience. And guess what they think they have found. The Holy Spirit. Irony again. How can one be so filled with the Spirit and so impatient? One can't. Deceit is having its way, its day and its say. Impatience is not of the Spirit.

False joy is no different. Materialism can be given much credit here. As a matter of fact "credit" is almost a pun in that sentence. Buy it now and pay on it the rest of your life doesn't appear to be such a bad deal. Temporary often has that appeal. Yet after twenty-four months the shine is lessened, the rust is noticeable and the rattle is somewhere — we just can't tell exactly where. And now we have an average item in our garage or our den and only thirty-six payments to go. What joy. Or rather, what joy?

Filled with the Spirit makes no earthly sense. Yet it is the earthly sense that traps us every time. It promised us great and wonderful life, only to disappoint and not keep up its end of the deal. The kingdom of God is real life. No half-hearted, half-filled person is in proper alignment.

Filled with the Word and, yet, no presence of the Holy Spirit is a life that is a lie. That life is not filled with the Word. It is filled with humanistic, earthly substitutions. It is filled with Bible references. How many Christians (?) there are who are critical, nervous, fearful and pessimistic — all in the name of the Lord.

Be filled to the brim with the Spirit of God. He has given. We are free to receive.

CHAPTER 4

THE PARALLEL ABILITY

Jesus was actually stranded without the Spirit of the Father. He was devastated on the cross as God turned His back and walked away from the sin Jesus had become — II Cor. 5:21. Psalms 22 reveals the Son as completely exasperated when forsaken by the Father.

However, it is to be accented that as long as this human was in tune with the One above he could bear fruit. If he didn't have "Spirit - help" he declares himself as empty and stranded as any person without God. "Apart from the Father I can do nothing." That is how totally dependent Jesus, the Son of Man, was upon the Spirit power.

We are no different — rather, we are the same! Jesus told us, "Apart from me, you can do nothing. He who bides in me and I in him, he bears much fruit (Jn. 15:5)."

We have been of the nature to knock our knuckles red to win souls than to so abide in Jesus that the Spirit might naturally and easily let fruit come about. From the beginning a principle has been so: "Wait for what the Father has promised" (Acts 1:4) and then "you shall be my witnesses."

The reason we are failing in the realm of evangelism is that we don't have the steam to witness because we have approached the world with humanistic salesmanship. Honesty will perceive our failures in several areas of Christian stewardship. Yet, the good news — the too good of news to be true — is that there is an honest reason to hope for and to pursue success in the Jesus — style. Let us, therefore, expand these thoughts that we might gain valuable insight to the thrill of effective kingdom living.

He Is Always "Yes"

Eventually each of us will find himself handicapped in Christian service by physical limitations. Such has been the entire message of Holy Writ. That's the point. Spirit living yields Spirit fruit in Spirit orchards when a fleshly one will undergo a Spirit transplant. Our nature is transformed and elevated to higher standards to activity and accomplishment.

Able? In the flesh-nature the answer is "sometimes" followed with an immediate lowering of the head while it is whispered, "And sometimes not." Yet, in the Spirit nature, the response is always, "Yes." "For the Son of God, Christ Jesus, who was preached among you by us — by me and Silvanus and Timothy — was not yes or no, but is yes in Him. FOR AS MANY AS MAY BE THE PROMISES OF GOD, IN HIM THEY ARE YES; wherefore also by Him is our Amen to the glory of God through us."

Continuing with this quote, catch the elements — rather the Element — as to how and why this is true. "Now He who establishes us with you in Christ and anointed us is God, who also sealed us and GAVE US THE SPIRIT IN OUR HEARTS as a pledge (II Cor. 1:19-22)." Yes, it is you and me who

51

are able — able because we are indwelt by Him who is able (Eph. 3:20).

Again, re-emphasis must be made that Jesus who is "God in limited-by-the-flesh clothing" explained one of the reasons he is a normal person. "Truly, truly, I say to you, the Son CAN DO NOTHING OF HIMSELF, unless it is something he sees the Father doing. . . (Jn. 5:19)." Surely Jesus doesn't mean that! He could do nothing? No thing? Yes that's the message. He became human to demonstrate how inadequate flesh-style could conquer such restrictive boundaries once the interior is energized with the Above Standard.

"Apart from Me you can do nothing (Jn. 15:5)." Nothing. The same amount of "no thing" that was with him in the flesh. His statement stands firm. With God, he can get it done. With God, we can do it. Apart from God, Jesus is broken down alongside the road of doing. Apart from God, we sit stranded with wishful eye upon those trafficing steadily past us on the highway of accomplishment. And we wonder why we aren't accomplishing anything worthwhile and effective.

The message is on the lips of the Christ. With God the inadequate becomes totally and always adequate (II Cor. 3:4-6). With such expression let it be noted that it was he who said his followers would get more done than He did. "Truly, truly, I say to you, he who believes in Me, the works that I do shall he do also; and greater works than these shall he do; because I go to the Father (Jn. 14:12)." Can He be serious? Yes, and, it is statements like these that make this book a "must" from my heart to yours. Friend, do be astounded and overwhelmed by his statement. One must believe him in John 14:12 as happily as we believe him in John 3:16!

Who Can Do More Than Jesus?

How can this be? First, it is true because of the reality as to the total humaness of Jesus. He was not the exception to humanity. He was the norm. He was common and ordinary in that he experienced being a full and dependent earthling. Dependence is central here. WITHOUT GOD? NOTHING. CASE CLOSED. WITH GOD? ALL. CASE CLOSED. For who? For Jesus; and as it is for Jesus it is for us.

Second, it is true because of the Spirit. Notice his phrase at the end of John 14:12, "because I go to the Father." Greater works because. When God-in-the-flesh returns to his heavenly position then God-in-the-Spirit descends, not only to hover over mankind as one giant helicopter but to be a "live-in." The Spirit moves to the inside. Thus, God has covered life for us.

He covered the area of exterior, external living by the example of Jesus. Jesus was the "how to" of successful human living. Basically, he lead the way in training the body to submit to the Higher Life. Then, God covered the inside of living by sending His Spirit to indwell and function. Friend, neither higher technology nor advanced science will ever discover such a magnificent truth. God understands us inside and out! From such an observation one can see how we could be "totally" His. This is so beautiful it surpasses understanding in an overwhelming way. It's "too good of news to be true." Yet, it is all gospel!

Equipped for the task of productive living? Wonderfully so. Thank the Lord, too, that such furnishing is not uncomfortable, awkward or bulky like the armour David tried. The Spirit is a perfect fit. Our armour is easy, light and mobile. "But we have this treasure in earthen vessels, that the surpassing greatness of the power may be of God and not from ourselves. . . (II Cor. 4:7)."

We are earthen containers; and just like the container of Jesus, no less. Totally human. We are to be just us. Earthen, formed from dust, suddenly excuses no longer slip from our feeble lips. Rather it is power (II Cor. 4:7) and confidence (II Cor. 3:4) and love (Rom. 5:5) and discipline (II Tim. 1:7) and dynamic faith (II Cor. 4:13). This knowledge makes a Christian burst forth with a zeal that will not be turned back by the highest tides of discouragement and negative pressure.

It is you, my friend, that is more powerful than any nuclear plant. You contain the Invisible Force that out-lasts, out-lives and out-loves any enemy combatant. We are not average. Don't live another moment with the just-getting-by mentality. We are indwelt! We are co-God! We carry His type of strength.

Lift your sights of your nature, life and calling. Scripture says we are co-laborers with God (II Cor. 6:1). We read it. But do we fully believe it? Be encouraged to grow in this communion with Him.

Believers contain a "divine nature" (II Pet. 1:4). Divine. Be drawn to higher standards. Such will happen when we can accept the fact that we are on a first-name-basis, so to speak, with God. It is even more. It is a father/child relationship. He is in us.

We are in Him. . . close, inseparable.

Partners with God? As far as all-knowing? No. All-presence? No. All-powerful? No. All-able to do what He wants and needs to do through us at the moment? Yes. Consider the carnal servant who was a diligent follower of God. His fame will survive the ages. Yet, he angered God.

God:	"I will send you to Pharoah, so that you may bring My people, the sons of Israel, out of Egypt."
Moses:	"Who am I that I should go?"
God:	"I will be with you."
Moses:	"I wouldn't know what to say."
God:	"I will be with you."
Moses:	"What if they don't believe me?"
God:	"I will be with you."
Moses:	"But, I'm not very eloquent."
God:	"I will be with you."
Moses:	"I don't know. Isn't there anyone else that would go?"
God:	(Infuriated by the shallowness of this coward) "Is there not your brother Aaron the Levite? I know that he speaks fluently. And moreover, behold he is coming out to meet you; when he sees you, he will be glad in his heart."
	"And you are to speak to him and put the words in his mouth; and I, EVEN I, will be with your mouth and his mouth, and I will teach you what you are to do."
	"Moreover, he shall speak for you to the people; and it shall

come about that he shall be as a mouth for you, and YOU SHALL BE AS GOD to him."

So, efforts were made to obey. Events were mixed with doubt and frustration. The believing brothers were still found as mere men. . . questioning whether they were doing any good. Again in Exodus 7:1 God had to re-confirm His statement. "Then the Lord said to Moses, "See, I MAKE YOU AS GOD to Pharoah, and your brother Aaron shall be your prophet."

Therefore, let not the idea of being co-laborers with God be received as exaggerated, absurd and ridiculous. Do let it remove us from the pathetic and anemic error of excuse-ism that God found disgusting in Moses.

The term is to be viewed as a tightly interlinking bond of communion that we and He share. He is not a DISTANT relative. He is carried within our essence. He literally dwells within us. We are not neighbors to Jehovah. . . we are one with Him.

He Has A System . . . That Works!

Keeping in mind that it is the Lord who equips us, we must surely believe His wisdom is of the nature that He wouldn't mistakenly furnish His people with a system that would malfunction. It is God who is all-able so it must be our responsibility to be all-receptive by believing this good news code.

A special facet of the Christian productive unit empowered by the energy of the Holy Spirit is that of evangelism. Reaching out and sharing one's faith has been a brutal experience for the masses of disciples. On one hand there are those who pursue their neighbor with the zeal of a deer hunter, interested mainly in the trophy to show off his achievement. At the other extreme those are found burdened and beaten having the knowledge that they should be sharing Jesus, but helplessly intimidated. Furthermore, I don't believe the truth of effective witnessing is found somewhere camouflaged in the middle.

All can be lifted to a higher and better surface when alerted to the equipping of the Spirit. Even the ministerial trainees of Jesus were going nowhere without this same Force. "And gathering them together, He commanded them not to leave Jerusalem, but to wait for what the Father had promised. . . you shall receive power when the Holy Spirit has come upon you; and you shall be My witnesses both in Jerusalem, and in all Judea and Samaria, and even to the remotest part of the earth (Acts 1:4, 8)." Power and witnessing are simultaneous when the Spirit is on the scene. Why is this? Courage will never be strong in the human who has the will but has not the Spirit.

Peter had the will before the Holy Spirit was sent. In Mt. 26:33, "But Peter answered and said to him, 'Even though all may fall away because of You, I will never fall away'." By sunrise this one with outstanding and sincere ambition had withered at the hands of nameless and incidental passers-by. Ashamed and defeated he sobbed the morning away — Mt. 26:75.

Yet, after he had waited for the Spirit of promise — Acts 1:4, 8 — we read of an entirely new man. "But Peter, taking his stand with the eleven, raised his voice and declared to them. . .(Acts

2:14)." Again in Acts 4:8, "Then Peter, filled with the Holy Spirit said to them. . ." Silence is void, not of sound but of Spirit. Expression is afforded only because of courage provided by Him.

"Therefore I make known to you. . . no one can say, 'Jesus is Lord', except by the Holy Spirit (I Cor. 23:3)." "By this you know the Spirit of God: every spirit that confesses that Jesus Christ has come in the flesh is from God (I Jn. 4:2)." It appears that the non-believing world is overpoweringly intimidating. One can be at lunch with colleagues as discussion arises concerning the routine activities of life in general. Occasion for giving praise and credit to Jesus for his providing that open door or assisting in the recent pressures is at hand. Yet, it is my observation that the courage to express such faith can only originate from the Spirit that gave Peter newfound valor. Otherwise, we sit in silence.

Is this idea not reinforced by the words of Paul in I Corinthians 2:1 and :4? "And when I came to you, brethren. I DID NOT COME TO YOU WITH SUPERIORITY OF SPEECH or of wisdom, proclaiming to you the testimony of God. . .and my message and my preaching were not in persuasive words of wisdom, but in demonstration of the Spirit and of power." Again in II Corinthians 4:13 it is emphasized that as some in the past spoke with gallantry we can do the same because we have the same spirit of faith.

Once more the human Paul said, "Pray on my behalf, that utterance may be given to me in the opening of my mouth, to make known with boldness the mystery of the gospel, for which I am an ambassador in chains; THAT IN PROCLAIMING IT

I MAY SPEAK BOLDLY, AS I OUGHT TO SPEAK (Eph. 6:19, 10)." It becomes obvious that momentum and resoluteness of expression of faith is enhanced solely by the indwelling God. We must, must, must pursue faith that we can be as forthright in expressing the good news we experience.

Equipped for the task of evangelism by the power of the Holy Spirit? That is why he was sent in the first place — that believers be equipped to witness. Acts 1:8, "...but you shall receive power when the Holy Spirit has come upon you; and you SHALL BE MY WITNESSES both in Jerusalem, and in all Judea and Samaria, and even to the remotest part of the earth."

Wisdom too, can be gained from the incite of the broken psalmist as he spoke to God. "Create in me a clean heart, O God, and renew a steadfast spirit within me. Do not cast me away from Thy presence, and do not take Thy Holy Spirit from me. Restore to me the joy of Thy salvation and sustain me with a willing spirit. THEN I WILL TEACH TRANS-GRESSORS THY WAYS, AND SINNERS WILL BE CONVERTED TO THEE (Psalms 51:10-13)."

Being a teacher of transgressors is not a matter of education (Acts 4:13), but is a matter of conficence by believing. It is not a matter of knowing what verse to share. It is a matter of believing the Spirit works within self. One can have all of the right answers and, yet, be so ineffective. Why? Absolutely no reliance upon the Spirit will always be the answer.

The written word offers a monumental challenge to the human mind when it insists that the invisible Spirit of God dwells with the visible tabernacle of man. To be productive from the Source within makes no earthly sense. It does, however, draw the disciple to be thoroughly and adequately equipped for the task.

Are we honest to assess parallel ability of the Spirit within Jesus and the Spirit within us? Yes, we are accurately honest. What is the greatest supernatural feat of His entire life? It was not the changing of the water nor the walking on it. It was. . .the resurrection.

My friends. . .scripture says that due to the Holy Spirit WE WILL DO THE SAME. The greatest and most profound move in history will be identically matched by us!

Parallel ability? It surely looks that way, doesn't it?

CHAPTER 5

THE PARALLEL DIRECTION

The Spirit was involved in the birth of Jesus; the baptism of Jesus; the declaration of the sonship of Jesus; the equipping of Jesus for the tasks and the filling of Jesus. In each of the previous chapters it has been resolved that each step was deliberate to show us the way. This chapter will approach another of the "Jesus did so we can" principles. The topic of him not calling the shots on his own, but being led by the Spirit is one that will make no earthly sense.

The Spirit impelled Jesus to go into the wilderness (Mk. 1:12). He was led about by Him through the duration of the wilderness venture (Lk. 4:1). This is true of the Son of Man. Too, this is the "Word become flesh" paving the way for us. Having received this same Leader we are to follow the trail.

"There is therefore now no condemnation of those who are in Christ Jesus. For the law of the Spirit of life in Jesus has set you free from the law of sin and of death. For what the Law could not do, weak as it was through the flesh, God did: sending His own Son in the LIKENESS of sinful FLESH and as an offering for sin. He condemned sin in the flesh, in order that the requirement of the Law might be fulfilled in us, who do no walk according to the flesh, BUT ACCORDING TO THE SPIRIT."

"For those who are according to the flesh set their minds on the things of the flesh, BUT THOSE WHO ARE ACCORDING TO THE SPIRIT, THE THINGS OF THE SPIRIT. For the mind set on the flesh is death, BUT THE MIND SET ON THE SPIRIT is life and peace. . .you are not in the flesh but the Spirit, IF INDEED THE SPIRIT OF GOD DWELLS IN YOU. But if anyone does not have the Spirit of Christ, he does not belong to Him (Rom. 8:1-6, 9, 10)."

We are to live according to Spirit direction. Location? The guidance is to come from God from within. Anyone who has difficulty in considering this is generally one who is legalistic in his opinions. Such is the enormous battle of these verses in Romans 8 and, also, in the seventh chapter: Law versus Spirit — legalism versus freedom. One makes earthly sense while the other never will.

(Let it be noted while we are here that Romans 8:9 documents the Holy Spirit, the Spirit of God and the Spirit of Christ as One and the Same. The very thought that moved me from the legal view that the Holy Spirit did not operate in my life was to realize that I believed that God did. How could God direct my life in any other form than spirit form? He is spirit.)

The statement in Romans 8:1-6ff concludes that sons of God are led by the Spirit — v. 14. Christians are to be spirit led. Humanity can be divided into the Christian camp and non-Christian camp. The Christian segment can be divided into spirit-led or law-led. Spirit-led sets the mind upon invisible activity. Besides those passages of Romans 8:5, 6, consider these. "Set your mind on things above, not on the things that are on earth (Col. 3:2)." "We look not at the things which are seen, but at the things which are not seen; for the things which are seen are temporal, but the things which are not seen are eternal (II Cor. 4:18)."

Things above, unseen, eternal are all connected to Spirit qualities. All live. . .endlessly. Things below, seen, temporary are all connected with law. All will end. . .die. The Spirit gives life. The law kills. To be Spirit-led is to concentrate upon the non-ending feature of creation.

A law-led mind is pursuing death from the outset because it gives attention to the tangible. Everything tangible ends. The mistake of those in Luke 18:9 was that they trusted in that which would end. . .themselves. "And He told this parable to certain ones who trusted in themselves that they were righteous, and viewed others with contempt."

". . .and may be found in Him not having a righteousness of my own DERIVED FROM THE LAW, but that which is through faith in Christ, the righteousness which comes from God on the basis of faith (Phil. 3:9)." Note the seen vs. unseen and death vs. life theme in this brief statement.

The law-guided one operates on right and wrong, good and bad, black and white rules. Not only is there no room for the "70 x 7" love of Jesus, law abiding citizens of the church often cannot afford the "7 times" forgiveness that Peter ridiculously posed as the answer. No. Usually such a narrow and "always right" person will find that three repeats of the same offense — not 7; not 70 x 7 — has pushed to the limit of mercy. Such a one is

63

found on the back porch bemoaning to God, "I have been faithful to observe every command and you've never let me do fun things with my friends." Lk. 15:29. Poor baby.

Led by the Spirit is much more than doing right and avoiding wrong. It is being. Being in Christ, free, saved, able, blessed, rich, justified, gentle, patient, etc. Law-people have trouble being any of these. The Holy Spirit leads us to accept these qualities. But our own determination will never "be" any of the above. It is only as the Spirit gives this to us, that we attain such noble standards.

"But if you are led by the Spirit you are not under the Law (Gal. 5:18)." "But the fruit of the Spirit is love, joy, peace, patience, kindness, goodness, faithfulness, gentleness, self-control; against such things THERE IS NO LAW (Gal. 5:22, 23)." God and sin do not co-exist. Spirit and law will not either. It must be pointed out that even though all people, legalistic and even non-Christian, can display all of the above mentioned fruit of the Spirit at times, there is still a huge difference. Only the Spirit-led one can withstand the heat under fire.

Jesus, led by the Spirit, had loving and gentle compassion for his enemies at the cross. Stephen, being full of the Spirit, followed the path blazed by Jesus as he was being stoned to death in Acts chapter seven. We are called upon to suffer, uttering no threats, loving those who hate us, all the while entrusting ourselves to the God who judges rightly — Mt. 5:38-48.

"For you have been called for this purpose, since Christ also suffered for you, leaving you an example for you to follow in His steps, who committed no sin, nor was any deceit found in His mouth; and while being reviled, He uttered no threats, but kept entrusting Himself to Him who judges righteously; and He Himself bore our sins in His body on the cross, that we might die to sin and live to righteousness; for by His wounds you were healed (I Pet. 2:21-24)."

Since we are to follow such an example, let us rephrase this text to see our true position in the kingdom:

"We are following His example, although we didn't originate the problem; while being accused, we will not be defensive; while suffering, we will not breathe threats, but simply trust God to make everything work out; and we ourselves bear their sins in our body on the cross we take up daily that they might die to sin and live to righteousness; for by our wounds they are healed." Although we do not literally forgive sins — only Jesus does — we have the authority to forgive one another. Our friends and neighbors and enemies will find the road to eternity open when we can maintain our lifestyle upon the cross.

Even our enemies would find us patient, gentle, kind, etc. . .all the fruit from our carcasses borne by the Spirit within.

True spirituality is never proven until it is in the presence of its enemy. Anyone can do good when there is no opposition. The rubber meets the road when mistreatment presents itself. It is at this point that humanity cannot continually, successfully bring forth patience, gentleness, etc. We must call upon the Spirit through faith to go to work.

Many a preacher has resigned for legitimate

reasons. Elders, deacons, teachers, bus workers and others have done the same. Yet, let it be cautioned that many may have quit because they were not relying upon the Spirit. It is fairly easy to detect. In the first place it is nestled in the arms of contempt for others — Lk. 18:9. Linked to such disdain is impatience, hatred, bitterness, resentment, envy, disgust; all deeds of the flesh. None are produced by the Spirit.

"Who among you is wise and understanding? Let him show by his good behavior his deeds in the gentleness of wisdom. But if you have bitter jealousy and SELF-ish ambition in your heart, do not be arrogant and so lie against the truth. This wisdom IS NOT THAT WHICH COMES DOWN FROM ABOVE, but is earthly, natural, demonic."

"For where jealousy and selfish ambition exist, there is disorder and every evil thing. But the wisdom FROM ABOVE is first pure, then peaceable, gentle, reasonable, full of mercy and good fruits, unwavering, without hypocrisy. And the seed whose fruit is righteousness is sown in peace by those who make peace (Jas. 3:13-18)."

How, my friend, does wisdom flow from above. Is it not something that was given all at one time in the past? No. Such can be documented by James 1:5 where any who lacks wisdom is told to ask and God will give it. It flows from above in spirit form.

Being led by the Holy Spirit of God does not involve our "doing" things as much as it required our "letting" Him work in us. The Spirit will bear fruit in us if we will let Him by our faith. The spies could not enter the promised land because they would not let it be possible. All they had to do was believe. Yet they calculated "right and wrong" conditions concluding that they could not enter according to fleshly limitation. They were not LED BY GOD but were setting their minds on the "SEEN". The problem was that God never asked them to do or refrain from doing. He only wants them to believe His promise.

So it is with us. Listen to the negative reporters in the church. Whine, moan, complain. A confident person in the Spirit? No, always one with criticism that people could "do" more or "do" better or keep from "doing" this or that. Again, one can see in them the lack of Spirit fruit. Instead of patience it is impatience. Instead of gentleness it is edginess. Instead of self-control it is the strong insistence that others be controlled.

". . .we have not ceased to pray for you and to ask that you may be filled with the knowledge of His will IN ALL SPIRITUAL WISDOM AND UNDERSTANDING, so that you may walk in a manner worthy of the Lord, to please Him in all respects, bearing fruit in every good work and increasing in the knowledge of God; STRENGTHENED WITH ALL POWER, ACCORDING TO HIS GLORIOUS MIGHT, FOR THE ATTAINING of all steadfastness and patience; joyously giving thanks to the Father, who has qualified us to share in the inheritance of the saints in light (Col. 1:9-12)."

It makes no earthly sense but the Spirit does work within us. It is clearly stated in this text that we are given strength to attain steadfastness and patience. Meaning? One can't keep going on his own will-power. We are living in the kingdom of all kingdoms — God's. We must have help from the

Power. We do! Let Him function within our earthen vessel. By faith, let Him lead!

If the Holy Spirit is operating in Christians today then isn't it of necessity that He employ identical signs and wonders of old? No. It is not up to the believer to coerce the Spirit to provide us with any specific ability. We are to be open to His capacity. That's the way it was in the early stages of the church. "But one and the same Spirit works all these things, distributing to each one individually just as He wills (I Cor. 12:11)." We are filled and led by that very same, only, one Spirit (:12).

Some of us do not believe He operates in all of the areas He did in the beginning because they are not necessary. Yet due to our conviction we have thrown the baby out with the bathwater. Shut Him out, off and down and then there won't be any Holy Spirit error. That in itself is error. It is as much up to us, as it is those who desire every gift, to be open to one concept through faith. We must let the Spirit use us as He wills. Immediate challenge is present because the only way one can do so is to die to self.

If it is more important to you to preserve the church to the standards of 1950 then you are very likely not open to the Spirit. You have your own selfish ambition. Remember what James 3 says of that. Disorder and every evil thing arises.

If it is an issue with you that the posture of the church be similar to the style of Luther, Campbell, Lipscomb or Calvin, then it is dangerously possible you will tell the Spirit what He can and cannot do. Major change must be made by us; not others. We must repent — that strong — of our unbelief in the Spirit area. I have been wrong. It is not sound doctrine to quench the Spirit. It is violation of scripture.

We must yield to instruction in order that we might be accurate in this matter. The Spirit is God. Consider the latter days of II Timothy 3 and you'll find religious people dead-set in organization but powerless. Dead-set is to be dead! Dead churches can find Life! Weak pulpits can be aroused! Stale Bible classes can be revived! Anemic ministries can be refreshed! All due to one Element.

Cattle will walk a long way for salt. They won't travel twenty feet for a block of pure, unadulterated cardboard. People will put out sacrificial efforts to learn of the true value of the Spirit. They won't bother to set down to another meal of "cardboard Christianity".

Apparently the way to let the Spirit lead depends a lot upon eyes of faith. Evidently the trust of God-guidance is positioned upon the perspective of each believer. In itself, a believer is one who used a unique set of eyes. Truly this makes no earthly sense. Yet from the beginning this has been a significant mystery.

Adam and Eve were not blind people. They could see the tree and the garden. The moment sin abruptly entered the scene another set of eyes were opened. This sighted couple suddenly saw that they were naked. "The eyes of both of them were opened. . .(Gen. 3:7)." Self-consciousness remains strong since that day.

I believe it is the effort of God through the Spirit to restore mankind back to original sight — the first set of eyes. We are to walk by faith, not by sight (II Cor. 5:7). Faith sees from the heart. Faith sees what cannot be seen by "earthly sense" eyes. Such is more daring and spectacular than any special effects glasses used to see the outlandish dimensions of extremely creative movies. Also, the most high-powered lens cannot pick up on the invisible matter that faith can see.

". . .while we look not at things which are seen, but at the things which are not seen; for the things which are seen are temporal, but the things which are not seen are eternal (II Cor. 4:18)." Christians are led by the Spirit conclusively in that we are able to see secret signals. This is the reason the Holy Spirit makes no earthly sense. Earthly sense can't see the invisible.

Verification of this seen/not seen world is revealed in an incident of II Kings 6:15-17. "Now when the attendance of the man of God had risen early and gone out, behold, an army with horses and chariots was circling the city. And his servant said to him. 'Alas, my master! What shall we do?' So he answered, 'Do not fear, for those who are with us are more than those who are with them.' Then Elisha prayed and said, 'O Lord, I pray, OPEN HIS EYES THAT HE MAY SEE.' AND THE LORD OPEN-ED THE SERVANT'S EYES, AND HE SAW: and behold, the mountain was full of horses and chariots of fire all round Elisha."

The leading of the Spirit is brilliant in its format. He privileges us to view directly into the undetectable. Our pursuit takes on the Masterminded dimension. By faith we can get a grip on the total life. So for you, my friend, I quote Paul who was blinded once in order that he might find real life. "I pray that THE EYES of your heart may be enlightened, so that you may know what is the hope of His calling, what are the riches of the glory of His inheritance in the saints and what is the surpassing greatness of His power toward us who believe (Eph. 1:18, 19)."

If one is to be led by the Spirit, one is of necessity called to search with new eyes. Practical? Friend, it will be terrific if we could have a new outlook on life. That is precisely what the Holy Spirit provides.

Name the person more powerful than Jesus. Yet, even he credits his success to the Spirit (Mt. 12:28, Lk. 11:20). Is it feasible to apply such credentials to other humans. . .like us? Certainly. If not, then he lied when he said, "Truly, truly I say unto you, he who believes in Me, the works that I do shall he do also; and greater works than these shall he do; because I go to the Father (Jn. 14:12)."

"And I will ask the Father, and He will give you another Helper, that he may be with you forever; that is the spirit of truth, whom the world cannot receive, because it does not behold Him or know Him, but you know Him because He abides with you, AND WILL BE IN YOU (Jn. 14:16, 17)."

We are not given the Holy Spirit for no reason; nor little reason; nor useless reason. We must have Him within that we might be transformed from pathetically weak to magnetically powerful. "And such confidence we have through Christ toward God. Not that we are adequate in ourselves to consider anything as coming from ourselves, but our adequacy IS FROM GOD, who also made us adequate as servants of a new covenant, not of the letter, but of the Spirit; for the letter kills, but the Spirit gives life (II Cor. 3:4-6)."

71

To be inadequately adequate or adequately inadequate makes no earthly sense. To welcome within our inadequacy the residence of the Adequate One we become energetically useful. "But we have this treasure in earthen vessels, that the surpassing greatness of the power may be of God and not from ourselves (II Cor. 4:7)." We are intentionally called in our earthen plainness to serve that the strength might not be self-produced. Such self-mustering efforts are always too little. Christians have a task set before them that cannot succeed by the "man-power" available.

Were we intentionally called because of our simple lack of acclaim? "For consider your calling, brethren, that there were not many wise according to the flesh, not many mighty, not many noble; but GOD HAS CHOSEN the foolish things of the world to shame the wise, and God has chosen the weak things of the world to shame the things which are strong, and the base things of the world and the despised. God has chosen the things that are not, that He might nullify the things that are, that no man should boast before God (I Cor. 1:26-29)."

Stamped at the top of the cover of my Bible is, "Power is perfected in weakness". I have that placed there to remind me when the butterflies won't fly in formation within my stomach that such nervousness can be transformed into true confidence as the Spirit lives well in clay vessels.

"And He has said to me, 'My grace is sufficient for you, for power is perfected in weakness.' Most gladly, therefore, I will rather BOAST ABOUT MY WEAKNESSES, that the POWER OF CHRIST may DWELL IN ME. Therefore I am well content with weaknessess, with insults, with distresses, with perecutions, with difficulties, for Christ's sake; for when I am weak, THEN I am strong (II Cor. 12:9, 10)." The well-trained, self-confident person ready to roll for the King or the discouraged, unimpressive one who believes in the potential of Jesus — which did God choose? Now you know. Earthly sense? Exactly backward to it!

"For indeed He was crucified because of weakness, yet He lives because of the power of God. For we also are weak in Him yet we shall live with Him because of the power of God directed toward you (II Cor. 13:4)." Jesus, the earthen human vessel was weak. So weak was he that he died. Yet, today, he lives. Why? Not because of himself. He lives because of the power of God who raised him. Romans 8:32 says the Spirit who raised Jesus dwells in you. Once again it must be stressed that we are to be of certain confidence when we understand that Jesus relates to our very inability. He became flesh on purpose for a purpose. He paved the way for us to convert the flesh to power. These Jesus/us parallels are consistently promoted by the inspired word of God.

Does the Holy Spirit function from the interior of man? Yes. "For this reason I bow my knees before the father, from whom every family in heaven and on earth derives its name, that He would grant you, according to the riches of His glory, to be STRENGTHENED WITH POWER through His Spirit IN THE INNER MAN (Eph. 3:14-16)." The Holy Spirit is the total power of the disciple. Without Him we are a dead carcass. With Him we gain strength — invisible, direct strength — to do kingdom work.

It is startling to realize the "power" struggle involved in believing the Spirit performs in the common one today. As a matter of fact it is more than a struggle; it is all-out war. We are aware of two kingdoms — the material one and the invisible one. Each is kept alive by its own source. The materialistic world is kept alive by money. Money is its reason, breath, talk and drive.

What would the business world be like without money? Department stores wouldn't have a purpose. Why open the doors if not to make a sizeable profit? So let's suppose we do eliminate revenue from the materialistic world. Doors to business open; but no one knows why. There will be no commission — there is no money. Abruptly one can conclude that without its source there is immediately no direction, reason nor motivation. Keep the doors open for business? Yes. But why? One can only fumble for a decent answer.

And, so it is with the church. The invisible kingdom has as its power the Holy Spirit. Remove the Spirit from the premises and the church has no reason to open its door. A spiritless congregation is left only with routine and traditional ways of doing things. Instant monotony sets in. Classes can be conducted with great gusto. However little change can be recognized in the students. Sermons can be delivered with driven enthusiasm only to be approved by the passers-by at the door. What is lacking? The Spirit.

Let there be deep warning as to the significant battle for position between these two worlds. It was not a mere devotional courtesy offered when he said, "No one can serve two masters; for either he will hate the one and love the other, or he will hold to one and despise the other. You cannot serve God and mammon (Mt. 6:24)." Friend, this is blatantly accurate. As an evangelist I can tell you the topic that is most dreaded by the church visitor (and many a church member). It is "giving."

"Wouldn't you know it!" "I haven't been to church for six years and the one Sunday I do go the preacher talked on giving." Why the rub? Why such a sensitive irritant? Because two kingdoms are at war. Each has its source of motivation. Give me a dead church and I'll show you one that is legalistic and spiritless. Show me a congregation alive and I'll show you one that is motivated by the resourcefulness of the Holy Spirit. Such power we have due to His presence. Such deadness we have due to His absence.

Employing the power God sends is not an option. It is a command. Have you ever heard the idea of speaking as if God were speaking? That is a magnificent verse only half quoted. Here's how it reads. "Whoever speaks, let him speak, as it were, the utterances of God; whoever SERVES, LET HIM DO SO AS BY THE STRENGTH WHICH GOD SUPPLIES; so that in all things God may be glorified through Jesus Christ, to whom belong the glory and dominion forever and ever. Amen (I Pet. 4:11)."

To be encouraged to speak where and how God does is exceedingly noble in effort. To make such a move is to operate by great faith and commitment. In addition, for me to serve by the power correlating to God's strength is no less faithful. To actually believe that Holy Spirit power reigns within "average-Connie-Christian" takes pure, vibrant faith. Faith? Yes, if one isn't careful he will surmise by the timid or uncourageous presence of another that he or she is not very able. Such evaluation is mistaken by the obvious OUTWARD appearance. Faith moves its eyes beyond the surface and sees the invisible at work. . .the Holy, Invisible Spirit of Christ.

"I pray that the EYES OF YOUR HEART may be enlightened, so that you may know what is the hope of His calling, what are the riches of the glory of His inheritance in the saints, and what is the SURPASSING GREATNESS OF HIS POWER TOWARD US who believe. These are IN ACCORDANCE WITH THE WORKING OF THE STRENGTH OF HIS MIGHT which He brought about in Christ when He raised Him from the dead. . .(Eph. 1:18-20)."

We are filled with the Spirit, directed by Him and empowered lavishly through Him. May our hearts see further according to Eph. 1:18. And may we not quit until we rid ourselves once and for all of being filled by worldly distractions and are overflowing with the Holy Spirit — Eph. 5:18.

CHAPTER 6

THE JEWISH PARALLEL

"And this is eternal life, that they may know Thee, the only true God, and Jesus Christ whom Thou has sent (Jn. 17:3)."

"You know neither Me, nor My Father; if you knew Me, you would know my Father also (Jn. 8:19)."

"You search the Scriptures, because you think that in them you have eternal life; and it is these that bear witness of me: and you are unwilling to come to Me, that you may have life (Jn. 5:39, 40)."

The Secret of the Spirit Unfolds

An earlier chapter included discussion about Jesus being human. The secret to understand the Spirit is held in the ability to understand that Jesus was: (1) the Son of God (Jn. 3:16) and (2) the Son of Man (Mt. 9:6). Rather casually it is stated by many of us Gentiles that everybody knows that Jesus was totally God and totally man. It has been a painful experience to discover such remarks are often not soberly believed.

An error looms large among several that Jesus was not totally human. Such a position ruins his purpose of Hebrews 2:14-18. It denies Phil 2:6-8. And, finally, the verses above of John 5:39, 40; 8:19; and 17:3 declares that if we don't know Him we have no life in us.

Jesus was ever like us for a reason. He demonstrated how a flesh-person can walk with the Spirit-God. It is not a side-by-side concept; but rather an intertwined relationship. "I do not ask in behalf of these alone, but for those also who believe in Me through their word; that they may all be one; even as Thou Father, are in Me, and I in Thee, that they also may be in Us; that the world may believe that Thou didst send Me. And the glory which Thou has given Me I have given to them; that they may be one, just as We are one;"

"I in Thee, and Thou in Me. . .and I have made Thy name known to them, and will make it known; that the love wherewith Thou didst love Me may be in them, and I in them (Jn. 17:20-23, 26)."

God in spirit form had dwelt in Jesus who was in flesh form. Jesus in turn was raised to the right hand that his Spirit might be in us. If we deny that Jesus was the same kind of participating flesh as we, the gospel is destroyed. Its news does not sympathetically understand its weak hearers.

The Jews made the identical mistake; only in reverse. The Jewish race could not accept Jesus as being of God: diety. Yet He was and is. Gentiles, however, must be careful not to reject his being of man. The Jews rejected his divine element. We are bordering on rejecting his humanity, Earthly sense? Not to the materialistic mind. He was divine as a human. . .simultaneously.

Read the comment of Matthew 21:33-40 that conveys a truly disastrous style. "Listen to another parable. There was a land owner who planted a vineyard and put a wall around it and dug a wine press in it, and built a tower, and rented it out to vinegrowers, and went on a journey."

"And when the harvest time approached, he sent his slaves to the vinegrowers to receive his produce. And the vinegrowers took his slaves and beat one, killed another and stoned a third."

"Again he sent another group of slaves larger than the first, and they did the same thing to them. But afterward he sent his son to them saying, 'They will respect my son.' But when the vinegrowers saw the son, they said among themselves, 'This is the heir; come, let us kill him and seize his inheritance.'"

"And they took him, and threw him out of the vineyard, and killed him. Therefore when the owner of the vineyard comes, what will he do to the vinegrowers?"

The next seven verses of scripture explain the mistake the Jews have made in rejecting the Son whom God had sent. Rejection of Jesus in any capacity--Godhead or human--is toying with eternal fire.

The Jews felt that it would be irreverent to their God to believe that Jesus was a part of God. Gentiles must be careful in that we may feel it be irreverent to Jesus to believe he was mere man. The Jews felt they would offend God. We feel we would belittle Christ.

Note an even more ironic observation. The Jews rejected Jesus' goodness because they could look at him and see he was human. Gentiles today may reject His humanity because we can't see him and, thus know him only as God. The Jews' faith was lacking here because they couldn't get past what they saw. Ours is lacking because we can't get past what we can't see.

The Jews said, "You are trying to make too much of him." The Gentiles say, "You are trying to make too little of him." The Jews didn't want him in jeans--but in king's robes. We don't want him in jeans either; nor in king's robes--but in heavenly ones.

The Jews retreat to Mosaic Law for pattern of living while the Gentiles hide with denominational code to be guided by man-made doctrine. Neither is suitable and both have missed the boat all because Jesus is both God and man. Such makes no earthly sense and therefore thrusts the bulk of religion into a quagmire of deadness or busyness. . .or both. The result will be same as the Jews. . .emptiness.

Does It Make That Much Difference?

The Jews this and Gentiles that! Is it that important of an issue? Look at the Jewish religion. Bottlenecked by tradition, its early leaders killed Jesus. Don't overlook this matter. It was not gangsterland that did God's Son in. It was God's fold: His own sheep (Mt. 12:14). Furthermore, we are not talking Mother Goose here. Friend, we are talking historical, revealed fact.

Today the Jews--in general--do not know Jesus as the Son of God. Full of religion? Yes. Full of religious dedication and activity? Yes. Full of salvation? No. Read again the opening verses of this chapter from the book of John. Gentiles, too, are up to their necks in commitment, busyness, indebtedness, etc. Yet, if they reject half of the Christ in that he was as human as we, then he is of no value.

The Holy Spirit's capacity will not focus properly for us if we fail to let Jesus be flesh. He had to be made like his brethren--Heb. 2:14-18. He is sympathetic to our weakness--Heb. 4:14-16. Yet, we ruin his very purpose of civilized entry by excusing oursleves when we say, "But he was part God and that's why he could accomplish what he did. Sure, if I were divine I'd be doing a lot more too."

Although Jesus was always of the divine capacity and participation he restrained and limited himself to human style. He walked by faith in his Father. . .our Father. He maintained the position of a believer. His feet were shod with leather; not galactical array.

He was so human he aged. The honest mortality of Jesus was never more pronounced than when he bled. If ore should have flowed from his veins — or any other substance — his authenticity as a person would be questioned. He had to share in flesh and blood, even to the extent of death, that he could whip the devil on his own court.

"Tell me again how earthly he was." Refer once more to Philippians 2:6-8, ". . .who although he existed in the form of God, did not regard equality with God a thing to be grasped, but emptied Himself taking the form of a bond-servant, and being made in the likeness of men. And being found in appearance as a man, He humbled Himself by becoming obedient to the point of death on a cross." (The fact that we have studied this verse earlier in the Spirit material makes no difference. We must review the Word again and again. Its truth will ever become self-evident.)

1. Taking the form: Became like us to the extent of arms, legs, skull

and even at one point...baby brain. He was like a person. He had even the appearance of such.

2. Humbled himself: A volunteer human in full respect. Yes, he could have chosen short-cuts to life and even by-passed the ancient ways. But...he didn't. He lowered himself by choice.

3. By becoming obe-dient: Being the "rank 'n' file" he was aforehand he could have entered giving orders and calling the shots. He was neither a brat nor a Brat! He was a person; obedient at that.

4. To the point of death: Why did he have to obey to die? Because my friend, he carried the power to skip it. For his brothers and sisters he did not default in his human style.

The Son of God/Son of Man was not an imitation person; nor a superficial one. He LEARNED to study. He LEARNED to pray. He LEARNED to obey. He LEARNED the role of a son, a man, a friend, a trainer. He LEARNED.

He was not Clark Kent-in-the-flesh. He was not robot. He was not illusion. He was not an exception to the being-like-us-rule.

He was always divine. Yet it is my opinion that he so confined himself to the earthen vessel that his link to his pre-existent home was profoundly channeled through the very same means we, too, have — the Holy Spirit.

It was the humble Friend who was led by the Spirit. He was dependent upon the Spirit. Jesus was divinely able to be so unable that the Spirit from above would make him re-able. Is that not the message for us in Ephesians 3:20? Its context is the Holy Spirit strengthening us (:16).

Looking at the Jewish rejection of his God part and the Gentile rejection of his human place, it leaves only one thing for those who still want to pursue God. Religious trivia is all that's left. We have majored in trivia and minored in faith. "What's legal here?" "How many trips did Paul go there?" "New Testament?"

None of that is wrong in itself. When the wholeness of the Christ is removed, though, trivia-mortis sets in. I believe, too, that both Jewish and Gentile religions are suffocating a slow death due to rote. The law kills and the Spirit gives life. Such a dramatic truth will never be found weak. No man can get to the Father but by Jesus. We must know him. He isn't an item. He's a friend. He isn't a statistic, a number, nor a piece of goods. He is a personable, personified, personalitized person!

Friend, how accepted will you be if you believe Jesus was totally human? By this I mean, how many will be in this camp of thinking with you? I believe this is a matter where few dare to tread, fewer dare to think and fewer there are who believe. How many Jews are there who believe Jesus is the

Son of God? Not many. That's about the same amount of Gentiles who believe him to have been in the flesh similar to us. The odd thing is that both groups believe he existed--only in opposite styles. The Jews believe he was a, catch this now, good man. We tend to believe he is God with just a touch of superficial manhood. We regard Him as superman shielded from all possibility of flaw or discrepancy.

Such a view lets us honor him with our lips while our hearts of faith, in that He truly understands our dilemma, are quite anemic.

What happens, then, if we choose to ignore Him in his full capacity? "But realize this, that in the last days difficult times will come. For men will be lovers of self, lovers of money, boastful, arrogant, revilers, disobedient to parents, ungrateful, unholy, unloving, irreconcilable, malicious gossips, without self-control, brutal, haters of good, treacherous, reckless, conceited, lovers of pleasure rather than lovers of God; holding to a form of godliness, although they have denied its power; and avoid such men as these (II Tim. 3:1-5)."

Jesus is the answer to the above enigma. To ignore Him is to deny the power. The power of Christ is the Spirit. If one wants to have church with no Spirit, then have at it. Be assured the decent and in order form can be attained. The power cannot be observed. . .because there is none in that setting.

What Is The Alternative?

If we fail to acknowledge Jesus in both of his phases, our alternative is to be a critical and judgmental body of so-called believers. Again, it was the Jewish Pharisees and scribes who stood around with a check-list on their clipboards of do's and don'ts. Their goal was to catch him wrong. That's how a mind operates when it's not turned to the full knowledge of Jesus.

An unbelieving mind will not necessarily denounce a professed faith. It may shift to the harsh and critical questioning of others. The Jewish leaders were incensed at the actions of the man from Galilee. Who did he think he was? God? Yet, their lack of belief did not curtail their fervor. Their zeal now had a target. . .to prove him wrong.

And, my dear friend, that's how it is with some today. There are quotation of scripture, observation of doctrine and information packaged on every tract rack. The lack of the Spirit does not curtail religious ferver. It merely redirects the targeting of itself upon any who approach the qualities of Jesus. The closer the resemblance the hotter the furnace. Such is no accident. It has always been the plan (Mt. 5:10-12).

". . .you are a letter of Christ, cared for by us, written not with ink, but with the Spirit of the living God, not on tablets of stone, but on tablets of human hearts. . .who also made us adequate as servants of a new covenant, not of the letter, but of the Spirit; for the letter kills, but the Spirit gives life (II Cor. 3:3, 6).''

A person can find death or life. . .in religion. Seek to know every jot and every tittle; seek the cut-and-dried, the black-and-white and you'll die. You'll die right in the middle of your bull-headed, stiffnecked, stubborn position.

Seek the mercy, peace, compassion of the Spirit

and you'll find yourself alive. . .as a gift. The gospel will be something to treasure; not something to guard. It will be fun; not sour. It will be inspiring; not depressing. It will breathe; not suffocate.

Where there is the total knowledge of Jesus there is a relationship. He is experienced from within. He moves from "on our case" to representing our case (1 Jn. 2:1, 2).

That We Be Full Of God

Before this chapter is closed, let us not overlook another significant matter. Let not this writing merely urge you to believe the full spectrum of the carpenter's son. By seeing him as one of us in the human realm, do see that he draws us to live in the God-realm.

He experienced life in the flesh and then God's Spirit in his flesh that we might follow suit. We are not to live "just us". We are to become more. We are to take on the divine nature.

"Grace and peace be multiplied to you in the knowledge of God and of Jesus our Lord; seeing that His divine power has granted to us everything pertaining to life and godliness, through the TRUE KNOWLEDGE OF HIM who called us by His own glory and excellence. For by these He has granted to us His precious and magnificent promises, in order that by them you might become PARTAKERS of the DIVINE NATURE, having escaped the corruption that is in the world by lust (II Pet. 1:2-4)."

We are heavily united in the divine participation of life. We are not mere honorary children. We are, too, Galileans and carpenter's sons--so to speak -- reborn by the Spirit, indwelt by the Holy God to make a difference as we symbolically spend our lives upon our cross that is similar to that of our brother and Lord.

"But as many as received Him, to them He gave the right to become children of God, even to those who believe in His name, who were born NOT OF BLOOD, NOR OF THE WILL OF THE FLESH, NOR OF THE WILL OF MAN, BUT OF GOD (Jn. 1:12, 13)."

"But we all, with unveiled face beholding as in a mirror the glory of the Lord, are being transformed into the SAME IMAGE from glory to glory, just AS FROM THE LORD, THE SPIRIT (II Cor. 3:18)."

". . .and to know the love of Christ which surpasses knowledge, that YOU MAY BE FILLED UP TO ALL THE FULNESS OF GOD (Eph. 3:19)."

". . .and that you be renewed in the spirit of your mind, and put on the NEW self, WHICH IS IN THE LIKENESS OF GOD has been created in righteousness and holiness of the truth (Eph. 4:23, 24)."

". . .and have put on the new self who is being renewed to a true knowledge according to the IMAGE OF THE ONE who created him--a renewal in which there is no distinction between Greek and Jew, circumcised and uncircumcised, barbarian, Scythian, slave and freeman, but Christ is all, AND IN ALL (Col. 3:10, 11)."

"For they disciplined us for a short time as seemed best to them, but He disciplines us for our good, THAT WE MAY SHARE HIS HOLINESS

(Heb. 12:10)."

It is true. Jesus partook of the lower nature that we might partake of the higher nature. He became a brother in the flesh that we could become his brother in spirit. He co-labored with our humanity that we could co-labor with His Father. To make Jesus less leaves us with less. In this perspective, the lower Jesus was the higher we became.

"He made Him who knew no sin to be sin on our behalf, that we might become the righteousness of God in Him (II Cor. 5:21)."

May the trade be complete.

CHAPTER 7

THE PARALLEL RESULTS

"For nothing will be impossible with God (Luke 1:37)."

Whoever made this statement better have his ducks in a row. When nothing is declared impossible a mighty area is ready to challenge. Yet, even our mortal efforts contain a hint of what we would consider inconceivable.

Man has developed ways to control blood pressure, transplant vital organs, send men to the moon, assemble automobiles that talk. Yes, and man can even perform operations to bring about a sex change. Before we ever get to God, man has conquered some impressive fields.

Let this simply elevate the reverent statement of Luke. If man can attain such measured results due to ingenuity, what could we do by faith in the Creator of man? We are called by God. This calling begs the shift from thinking according to the lower order. We are not only required to see new terrain via new eyes, we are able to do so.

To be reminded, "I pray that the eyes of your heart may be enlightened, so that you may know what is the hope of His calling, what are the riches of the glory of His inheritance in the saints and what is the SURPASSING GREATNESS OF POWER toward us who believe (Eph. 1:18, 19)."

By acknowledging the super-feats of man I'm

afraid that an incredibly important facet of God-involvement will be lost in the busy shuffle of being impressed. Perception of the Holy Spirit will not be limited to the unique or the rare occasion. His mighty power, again, matches and baffles what the earthly mind would count as big, or noteworthy of success.

The Spirit takes the common man with a common base and enables him to defy every set course of life from inadequacy to remaining confined to the all-destined grave. The Spirit gives us victory. Math formulas will not conquer the tomb. Faith in the Spirit of God will.

Of course the great Invisible Person affords us power that will accomplish the spectacular. We, by Him, are equipped to go where one cannot go, say what one is afraid to speak and to be what the community regards as impossible of being.

However, the true beauty of the Spirit, I think, is found in His operating within the simple. Peter was filled to the brim with the Holy Spirit. "Now as they observed the confidence of Peter and John, and understood that they were uneducated and untrained men, they were marveling, and began to recognize them as having been with Jesus (Acts 4:13)."

It is this "uneducated, untrained" frame that makes my heart leap with thanksgiving. Such a verse does not bring about collapse of instruction nor training. However, it does shine light on what we might consider hopeless disciples. Their very lack proved to be the motivation for marvel. Your very inadequacy is the source of others boasting in the Lord. "What's with Peter and John?", they could have asked. And their response was in the same breath, "The only thing I can figure out is that those guys must have been around Jesus."

People catch on when one spends time with the Master. There is such a "so shine" about His disciples (Mt. 5:16) that they actually do give the credit to the Father of spirits.

Once again this bumbling style of a man was found imprisioned (Acts 12:1-19). Once again God made His move in the face of the impossible. "So Peter was kept in the prison, but prayer for him was being made fervently by the church of God."

"And on the very night when Herod was about to bring him forward, Peter was sleeping between two soldiers, bound with two chains; and guards in front of the door were watching over the prison. And behold, an angel of the Lord suddenly appeared, and a light shone in the cell; and he struck Peter's side and roused him, saying, 'Get up quickly.' And his chains fell off his hands (Acts 12:5-7)."

The point? With the presence of God, not one thing shall be impossible.

Prayer remains to be pioneered. This frontier will find much room for new trails to be advanced. Our prayers are weak because His Spirit has been impounded. How can prayers be powerful if we allow not the Power? Thus we find ourselves with strong convictions, low-grade prayers and not enough fruit to call it a harvest.

We carry punch by faith. Look at the physical world of "super" strength. A Missourian had walked with the aid of two canes for years. His stooped position was always observed. Until! Until? Yes, there was that time that the tornado hit the house.

This crippled man stood up, ran to the next room and gathered his granddaughter in his arms. She was preserved from harm and he. . .had to have someone get his canes back in the kitchen so he could walk again!

The house caught fire. Filled with sudden power a slight-framed man unplugged the ringer washing machine loaded with water and laundry and he carried all this up the basement steps and set it upon the grass. It took three men to carry it back down to the basement. . .empty.

If this and countless other feats are performed daily by the human race due to the power of panic, why do we find it unthinkable when God advised that prayer could move a mountain? We, by faith, have the ability to call upon Force to be involved in our endeavors. We can't. But, He can through us!

We Are In This As Partners

It is God who dwells within the Christian in Spirit form. We co-labor with Him (II Cor. 6:1). Partners — close partners. With our faith and His ability, watch out world!

The nature and purpose of inner man benefits brought about by the Spirit is that God be free and able to work within the ordinary members of the church. We feeble ones are to be strengthened with power through His Spirit within us. As a result, Christ will dwell in our hearts. Having been rooted and grounded in love there becomes a comprehension that is understood by the universality of the rest of His children. It is such a deep-seated grasp that the love of Christ which surpasses knowing becomes known. When that love is known one becomes full of God. When full of God — then God is able to do exceeding abundantly beyond all that we ask or think ACCORDING TO THE POWER THAT WORKS WITHIN US — Eph. 3:16-21. Such profound ability of the conventional person is ever eye-catching. When noticed then immediate glory is given to God.

Why is this so? Because friends and acquaintances are not recognizing this new, Spirit-filled Christian according to the flesh — II Cor. 5:16. There is obviously a new dynamic part about this old friend. The Spirit changes us from within. Again, it is not what we wear but who we wear that determines if we are a Christian. When we wear Him and begin our adornment, not of jewelry but of love, we cannot keep our relationship with our Loved One hidden. He bursts forth from the center of our very being.

"I can do all things through Him who strengthens me (Phil. 4:13)." From where? Within. Confidence, listen to me now, is not found IN THE FLESH. It is found WITHIN THE FLESH. "If therefore there is any encouragement in Christ, if there is any consolation of love, if there is any fellowship of the Spirit, if any affection and compassion, make my joy complete by being of the same mind, maintaining the same love, united in spirit, intent on one purpose (Phil. 2:1, 2)."

"We. . .worship in the Spirit of God and glory in Christ Jesus and put no confidence in the flesh. . .(Phil. 3:3)."

"I, therefore, a prisoner of the Lord entreat you to walk in a manner worthy of the calling with which you have been called, with all humility and gentleness, with patience, showing forbearance to one another in love, being diligent to preserve the unity of the Spirit in the bond of peace (Eph. 4:1-3)."

The pursuit of unity cannot be attained by the flesh. It can be reached, though, by patience, by love, by gentleness, by peace which is not a standard of the mortal. It is the very fruit of the Spirit living inside the mortal.

A warehouse cannot put out newspapers. It can be loaded with a multiple range of items from storage of furniture, to food, to old cars. Yet it is desired that the warehouse be involved in producing the morning news. By the ambition of some the old building is cleansed from within. The clutter is moved out. Now what? Newspapers are desired; but such productivity isn't evidenced.

Then — when a printing press is positioned within the base structure of concrete and steel — the printed page comes from within the walls and its message will hopefully reach the person on the street. The building itself has some value but is not productive until the proper machinery is placed inside.

The flesh is of little value. But let it be willing to have the Spiritual Machine placed within its confines and love will be coming forth from the assembly line. We are to be rented warehouses. The Spirit desires to dwell in our personal tabernacle. He is a live-in. His presence means fruit — productivity — is on its way up and out. It is not our effort, but our willingness to share habitation with God in this body.

Look again at the opening of this chapter. Luke 1:37 is quoted confirming the exhilarating thought that all things are possible with God. That verse is in the context of Biblical revelation which truly does not make any earthly sense — the virgin birth.

It was the Holy Spirit doing an inside job that allowed the Son of God, son of man to be born. Mary was a good woman. That's all. It was not her ability to produce but her willingness to conceive that resulted in the most amazing story.

"And Mary said to the angel, 'How can this be, since I am a virgin?'" Full of reason and earthly sense, she brought up a quite exceptional question that should have stumped the messenger.

"And the angel answered and said to her, 'The Holy Spirit will come upon you, and the power of the Most High will overshadow you; and for that reason the holy offspring shall be called the Son of God.'" The Spirit does not make earthly sense but does produce significant, undeniable fruit. To this day there are those who do not believe in Jesus. Yet, their gravestone will be dated according to the year of his birth.

Earthly sense? No. God sense? Yes.

Mary's response is to be ours also. "And Mary said, 'Behold, the bondslave of the Lord; be it done to me according to your work.'" The ability does not register results. It is the willingness to yield to His Spirit within our interior that brings forth awesome production.

The Holy Spirit Implant

Mary was found pregnant as a result of the Spirit implanting the seed within her womb. As days and months followed the maturation of the seed delivered a healthy bouncing baby boy.

The beloved apostle authorized the following account. "And the Word became flesh, and dwelt among us, and we beheld His glory, glory as of the only begotten from the Father, full of grace and truth (Jn. 1:14)." The engrafted seed brought to full fruition was a person. It was Immanuel. Earthly sense isn't even in the picture.

Listen to me now, one of the most privileged phenomenon for our lives is to be found paralleled to this event. The seed is also to be implanted in our hearts. The originial language has as the word for seed the word "Sperma". We know it as sperm. The Holy Spirit delivered the sperm to the womb of the virgin. An infant child who ultimately grew to the stature of a man resulted. We are to receive that sperm into our hearts.

"Hear then the parable of the sower. When anyone hears the word of the kingdom, and does not understand it, the evil one snatches away what has been sown in his heart. This is the one of whom seed was sown beside the road."

"And the one on whom seed was shown on rocky places, this is the man who hears the word, and immediately receives it with joy; yet he has no firm root in himself; but is only temporary, and when affliction or persecution arises because of the word, immediately he falls away."

"And the one on whom seed was sown among the thorns, this is the man who hears the word, and the worry of the world, and the deceitfulness of riches choke the word, and it becomes unfruitful."

"And the one on whom seed was sown on the good soil, this is the man who hears the word and understands it; who indeed bears fruit, and brings forth, some a hundredfold, some sixty, some thirty (Mt. 13:18-23)."

It is within this parable that the word of God is shown as being planted in the hearts of men and women. What I want you to note in this segment is that the story of Mary parallels us. We are to receive the seed (sperm) in our hearts that Christ be formed in us. Yes, formed. In our human being the word is to become flesh. From each of us is to come forth the formation of the Christ.

Paul commented to the Galatian church, "My children, with whom I am again in labor UNTIL CHRIST IS FORMED IN YOU (Gal. 4:19)." The word sown in the heart is to ultimately take on the image of God's beloved and only begotten son.

"And so we have the prophetic word made more sure, to which you do well to pay attention as to a lamp shining in a dark place, until the day dawns and the morning star arises in your hearts (II Pet. 1:19)." The morning star that gradually evolves from within is none other than Jesus (Rev. 22:16) in spirit form.

When Mary gave birth, the word became flesh eventually walked the corridors of riches and ruins only to be pegged to an ugly and shameful cross. We are to give birth to the word become flesh. Only this time it is our flesh that he uses. He is formed from our inside out. Jesus borrows — or rents out — our arms, our ears, our feet, our lips, etc.

Before he was limited to two legs and two arms. Today he is limited by the amount of believing hearts. Before he could only be one place at a time. However, now he is vastly more aggressive in presence because the word (sperm) forms Jesus in our flesh. If he has 1000 disciples then he can be 1000 more places than when in his own tabernacle. If 1,000,000,000 followers — you get the picture.

Faith Not In Ourselves

From a slightly different angle let it be consistently voiced that it is the Spirit of God who makes us "All-able". Let me remind you of two marvelous statements pertaining to faith and Spirit.

"And my message and my preaching were not in persuasive words of wisdom, but in demonstration of the Spirit and of power, that your faith should not rest on the wisdom of men, but on the power of God (I Cor. 2:4, 5)."

Faith should not rest on earthly sense, but on God sense.

"But we have this treasure IN EARTHEN VESSELS, that the surpassing greatness of power may be of God and not from ourselves. . .(II Cor. 4:7)."

Let us get this message through our thick little heads. We are not to have faith in ourselves. We are to have faith in Him who dwells within ourselves. Ephesians 3:20 does not say "we" are able according to the power that works within us. No, it doesn't. It says He is able according to the power that works within us.

Our faith is that we can because of Him. It is not fair to us to keep stressing that we can because of ourselves. This is the difference between Theism and humanism. Theistic thinking makes no earthly sense. Humanistic thinking makes only earthly sense. Humanism says I can do all things. Theism says I am able to do all things because of Him.

Even some positive thinking can be snagged on the barbs of humanism. Christianity is more than salesmanship with a morning devotional at the beginning of the day. It is acknowledging that without the Divine, I can't. It's not a matter of knocking enough doors to meet or beat the odds. It is a matter of the Spirit which brings glory to Jesus and his church — Eph. 3:21.

"And such confidence we have — through Christ toward God (II Cor. 3:4)." I intentionally draw out that sentence that we might reason that we have every privilege of containing confidence. Such a trait is not there because of our self-image. It is present because of our Savior-image. If we could deny self and exalt Him we would find ourselves.

We are living in an age where it is not at all popular to mention anything contrary to self-esteem. Yet is is a matter of vital importance to the Christian to lose self in order that self be back — Lk. 9:24. Have we lost this issue? The reason we may have as much non-productivity as we do is that our people are unwilling to lose themselves; including their esteem. Not willing to be broken we become mired as a church in the constant meandering of the trifle. Why are so many who concentrate on their esteem so very low and inadequate when it comes to bearing fruit for the King. The answer is found in that we have tangled faith in oursleves with faith within ourselves.

Faith In The Invisible

"And all these things you ask in prayer, believing, you shall receive (Mt. 21:22)." Probably the greatest labor in the kingdom is to do this invisible work. To speak words to One we cannot see, asking Him to do that which we cannot see in order to bring about the results we desire — yet, cannot see.

Prayer is work. The reason it is so is not because of a weighty load but because of total reliability upon the spirit world. It is most difficult for the greatest of Christian worries because of that every imposing self — I'd rather do it myself."

Earthly sense bids for "handology." It believes its doctrinal core of a bird in the hand is worth two in the bush. Spirit sense believes that God can get the two and make the bush grow blackberries. Prayer launches into the invisible and comes out a winner.

Nothing Impossible

When we run with the crowd of Hebrews 11 we are in terrific danger of being faithful to the God of all gods. Faith is the assurance of things hoped for, the conviction of things not seen — 11:1. It is by faith we enter the world of Spirit. Eyes see beyond that which is seen — II Cor. 4:16-18. Have you ever noticed how many times Jesus told those who had ears to hear? Why did he do that? Because hearing, they didn't hear — Mt. 13:14-17.

We are called to see the invisible. God can create the sun and then find the man who by faith can stop the sun. He is willing to associate His Son's family tree with descendants like Rahab the harlot. Jehovah can do battle with the prince of the power of the air. And, too, He can make "ouwees" well for three year olds.

We must be awed that it is He who has chosen the foolish, the weak and the base to be instrumental alongside Him in the work of the Vineyard. But let us be awed with appreciation; not with surprise. For you see, He did the same of lowly Jesus. He used our brother as one mighty and noble. . .bond-servant. Jesus was only as much as the Holy Spirit was much in Him. We are no different in this brotherhood that Jesus established.

Let not the participation of lavish results be unexpected. It was our brother, Jesus, who said, "Truly, truly, I say to you, he who believes in Me, THE WORKS THAT I DO SHALL HE DO ALSO; AND GREATER WORKS THAN THESE SHALL HE DO; BECAUSE I GO TO THE FATHER (Jn. 14:12)."

When Jesus went back to the Father he did so that we might have results. If he goes back, then he will send the Spirit (:16). We will work well. The Spirit will no longer be confined to the body of Jesus. From now on He will be confined to the body of Christ; the church.

When you put the Father, the Son, the Spirit and the servant in one package, friend, you have got yourself a winner! That's what you are.

Lift up your eyes and see greater reaches of possibilities. It is not a matter of "I can" until it is a matter of "He is" within me. The results in our lives? Paralleled to those of the Christ. . .only more!

CHAPTER 8

THE PARALLEL CHALLENGE AHEAD

The Holy Spirit is the ultimate of controversy. He so completely makes no earthly sense that He baffles the complex mind. If man could control Him, package Him, measure Him or reduce Him to statistics on a 3x5 card, we would feel a whole lot better about this matter. Yet, when human brainpower tangles with that sphere which is beyond comprehension. . .believe me, the battle rages.

Other than the cross, nothing impacted society as stunningly as the grand entrance of the Royal Spirit on the day of Pentecost. He sent minds-a-spinning. He was overwhelming and overpowering. Lives were turned. Molds were broken. Mankind has never been the same.

As the dramatic and awesome presence of God was manifested, conflict of thought was simultaneous. The days ahead would find four classes of people:

1. Unbelievers who denied the Spirit.
2. Believers who denied the Spirit.
3. Believers who accepted the Spirit.
4, Believers who misused the Spirit.

Blend those four elements and the result is argumentative, not to mention disruptive confusion. For us today? Nothing has changed.

Is there a happy medium? If there is, who wants it? The disciple must not settle for anything less than accuracy pertaining to this Individual who dwells within. The Spirit's activity never conflicts with the Holy Word which He delivered (II Pet. 1:19-21). Nothing about God's kingdom is medium. All is excellent! Four mighty facets challenge the heart of every reader as the battle for clarity concerning the Holy Spirit continues to escalate.

The Challenge of Deception

Deception is the artwork of a thief. Yet, none of us can afford to neglect this as the success of fraud is to make the false appear to be true. The unique and crafty scheme of Satan is to delude. He is the master of imitators. He is as good at being phony as God is at being real. He is the ultimate of all con-artists.

Obviously, the magnitude of danger cannot be measured. The devil is strong in the art of offering flim-flam religion. It seems that what God can send, Satan can match. He constructs false teachers, christs, churches and doctrines. Too, he is able to match signs and wonders. For one to attest to anything as being true because they experience it doesn't make it true.

I passed down the hall and noticed the walls to the spare bedroom being pink in color. Seemed strange, didn't it? I never noticed that room being anything but white. It couldn't be pink. Yet, it was! I entered the room and checked more closely. Yes, it was pink all right.

The truth is it wasn't pink. The sun was entering room in such a way that it reflected the pink bedspread. By sundown the walls were incredibly restored to their true white color. If you would have put me on the witness stand before Perry Mason I would have sworn to the deceitful color — all because I saw it with my own eyes, Meaning? My eyes don't lie. Really? Well, I thought they didn't.

Arguments arise within the household constantly over someone thinking they said something in a definite way when the other party didn't hear it that way at all. Why is it that we can accept easily the idea that we do mistake the routine matters of life for what we thought we saw or thought we heard? And yet, when it gets to the discussion of the spiritual world we act as if there is no way we could have misconstrued what took place.

If Satan can copy christs, teachers and churches, he can certainly copy gifts of the Spirit. ". . .the one whose coming is in accordance with the activity of Satan, WITH ALL power and signs and FALSE wonders, and with all the deception of wickedness for those who perish, because they did not receive the love of the truth so as to be saved (II Thes. 2:9, 10)."

"You are of your father the devil, and you want to do the desires of your father. He was a murderer from the beginning, and does not stand in the truth, because there is no truth in him. Whenever he speaks a lie, he speaks from his own nature; for he is a liar, and the father of lies (Jn. 8:44)."

"Now there was a certain man named Simon, who formerly was practicing magic in the city, and astonishing the people of Samaria, CLAIMING TO BE SOMEONE GREAT; and they all, from the smallest to the greatest were giving attention to him, saying, 'THIS MAN IS WHAT IS CALLED THE GREAT POWER OF GOD.' And they were giving him attention because he had for a long time ASTONISHED THEM with magic arts (Acts 8:9-11)."

Elymas was providing profound illusions to keep people from the faith. Paul said, "You who are full of all deceit and fraud, you son of the devil, you enemy of all unrighteousness, will you not cease to make crooked the straight ways of the Lord (Acts 13:10)?"

All students simply must be reminded and alerted to the truth that the devil's trump card is professionally aligned on the spiritual, invisible battlefield — Eph. 6:11-16. The bulk of religion, I feel, wears the brand name of Jesus but has all the markings of counterfeit at bargain prices. From ultra-conservation to neo-miraculous we are being sold spiritual rot by the ton.

Vividly I recall the evening in my Dallas apartment when I discovered the message of Matthew 7:21-23. "Not everyone who says to me, 'Lord, Lord,' will enter the kingdom of heaven; but he who does the will of my Father who is in heaven."

"Many will say to Me on that day, 'Lord, Lord, did we not prophesy in your name, and in your name cast out demons, and in your name perform many miracles?' And then I will declare to them,. 'I never knew you; depart from Me, you who practice lawlessness.'"

I was stunned. It hurt to realize what this said. Evil unbelievers weren't the only ones to be cast into hell. Many followers of Jesus, to the extent of even doing respectable works in his name, will be — not can be, but will be misguided. Note that it is he who used the word "many" will say. . . .

Prophesy? Casting out demons? Miracles? All of no value if not according to the will of God. One must conclude that such people "did these things." It wasn't a matter of saying such maneuvers weren't happening. These works were being done; were seen by others; and were a reality in that they were taking place.

However, to say they are being done and that such proves it is God's divine will is to ignore this text. Too, this is in the context of how to know the false from the true. "Beware of false prophets, who come to you in sheeps's clothing, but inwardly are ravenous wolves (Mt. 7:15)." False prophets prophesy. False ways, manners, methods or people are not easily detected because of the cover — sheep's clothing.

One must, again, understand that such is not given attention to ridicule, attack or injure another's religion of personal conviction. It is intended that we all form a coalition against the crafty schemes of Satan in order that our minds be receptive to the glorious light of Jesus.

One must realize that I am not pulling the rug out from under the Spirit. He is true. I am conveying we have not only the right, but the responsibility, to test every spirit to see if it really is from God. To say it happened proves nothing. Did the happening come from God? That's what we all want to know. And we really want to know. This is not intended target practice on anyone but the devil. He will deceive.

The Challenge Of The Flippant

"Wearisome" exaggerated twenty times is the

word for the battle against the evil one. If he can't deceive maybe he could get us to accept anything and everything — which is an additional way of saying we've been deceived.

It is accurate to note that many, in my circle anyway, have been robbed of the relationship with the Holy Spirit. Laws have restricted. Unopenness has limited. Tradition has stifled. Now that the topic is beginning to leak out one must be prepared for the challenge.

It will be all too easy to swing the pendulum full arc. Shall we leap from the doctrines of no Spirit, no gift and no indwelling to the other extreme of everything that occurs is Holy Spirit motivated, supported and lead? Hardly. Such would only lead us to another dead-end alley of losing touch with spirit reality and actuality. When everything is Spirit-sent and everything is God-condoned and all is sugar-coated, the essence of Spirit direction has collapsed. God has given us a Spirit of POWER, LOVE and DISCIPLINE.

The Holy Spirit is not ooey and gooey. He is involved with discipline. He is not the support of every religious whim. He is not a "nut" loose in the halls of church houses or roaming the streets. He is more than a religious status symbol.

The Spirit of God bears fruit. He fits the guidance and instruction of Holy Writ. He equips for war against the force and power of the air.

The Challenge of the Complacent

The mediocre live in this house. The very theme of the segments of deception and flippancy drives some to this third category. What a bummer it is.

The Holy Spirit has been withheld from so many because church leaders feared where this might lead. There is no error greater than denying the spirit which is blasphemy.

Since some are deceived and others are space cadets it has been the earthly sense of several to scrap Him all together. Closeted He will give us no trouble and offer no threat. It is here that He is even referred to as an "it".

Disaster!

When there is no Spirit-presence there is no power. Where there is no Spirit there is death. Mediocrity is warm death. It makes the Master sick.

Many a church-goer can throw his shoulders back and say with confidence, "We never got into Holy Spirit error around here. The Bible is what we go by." Yes, and many a dead church there are because scripture — certain favorite verses — have been quoted and requoted. Everything was done decently and in order. So are funerals. More godly form with no power.

It is this type of believer that will have to answer the neglect of the command of Eph. 5:18. All are called to be filled with the Spirit. Which one? The only one — Eph.4:4-6 — the Holy Spirit.

The Challenge Of The Truth

Church steam can be gained due to the Spirit of God. Revised programs, new methods and old hat have all been tried to spur on new momentum. Nothing lasts outside of the Spirit participation. Cycles of "let's try this" call for more cycles. It is He who is stable.

We must not cost ourselves Spirit-power by playing-it-safe. The fulness of the church of Christ is marching beneath the banner of risk. To walk by faith and not by sight is to tread on daring waters.

There are those who rob banks. Yet, we don't shut down all banks for fear they will be hit. There are those physicians who are quacks. Yet, we do not avoid all doctors. Students fail and yet we don't close the schools. And the Holy Spirit is misunderstood and misused. How can we afford, though, to pretend He doesn't exist?

This book has put forth energy to claim that He does operate in the Christian. The writing intentionally has no references outside of scripture. Materials have not been compiled from the thoughts of others. It is my desire that the plain and ordinary like myself begin to think about Him. Let us be freed from the shackles of the debaters of this age to simply study the Spirit - delivered Word in order to discover what the Spirit guided the writers to say about Himself. May we be free to search. The truth is that liberty is found in Him. "Now the Lord is the Spirit; and where the Spirit of the Lord is, there is liberty (II Cor. 3:17)."

The truth is that the Spirit works in individuals as he wills — not as they will. "But one and the same Spirit works all these things, distributing to each one individually just as He wills (I Cor. 12:11)." As far as I can tell, it is the Spirit who determines what is needed as far as gifts. He is the enabler. Our duty is to respond to His direction rather than place an order-to-go.

The ultimate, the extreme, the most excellent mark of the indwelling is love. Enough has not been said about it. We do not hear too much about it. We cannot practice too much of it. We cannot get enough love.

Love embraces the sound, the certain and the accurate. One signal tells the world how to know who God's people are — the love signal (Jn. 13:34-35). It is love that is the excellent way (I Cor. 12:31).

If I have all the answers so as to win every argument, and yet have not love, I am a zero. If I win all debates and contend for the faith my entire life and yet do not have love — I have wasted my time. If I do more works than anybody else and sell my goods for missions and do not have love, I never got the picture.

Love is God.

We aren't talking about being courteous or nice. We are talking love when the circumstances aren't lovely. Anybody — athiest or believer — can love when all is going good. It is when times are rough and relationships are hurting that true love is tested. No one can love under pressure except by the Holy Spirit. We must have the Spirit bearing the fruit of love in us because we are called to win over the opposition. We can't do it on our own stamina.

Matthew 5:38-48 dispatches some pretty testy orders. Love your enemies. Pray for them in order that you may be sons of your Father who is in heaven. Loving the opponent is a test of sonship because it can't be done unless the Holy One is within.

What good is it if you love those who love you? Any athiest can do that. Get out there where the enemy is. Show your stuff! Let love be there in that setting. And why do you keep greeting with such friendliness those who are your friends? Speak to those who don't like you. Love the antagonistic and show the world you are a new and different nature.

We exult in the hope of the glory of God (Rom. 5:2). Cheer. Cheer. We also have the ability to exult in tribulation (:3). Really? Really? How? Why? Because the LOVE OF GOD has been POURED OUT WITHIN our hearts through the HOLY SPIRIT WHO WAS GIVEN to us (:5). The Spirit's reason to be within is to get a rascal of a person to be compassionate, merciful, gentle and kind to all neighbors. Behold, new things have come.

Society can see church buildings everywhere. It can verify that some have doctrinal footing. Others have status. Neighbors can see some churches grow. Others divide. But the element of truth is that when one loves under fire, you are looking at His child.

Church attendance doesn't make Christian claims valid. Being baptized doesn't settle the issue. Receiving the Holy Spirit at baptism so that one can love those who take advantage like stealing the coat or forcing to walk the mile — there is your Christian. Spirit love enables us to volunteer to be disadvantaged.

It is not in the Bible classrooms or the worship assemblies that relationship to the King is proven. It is waiting in line too long at the check-out counter, fighting snarling traffic and taking your new car in for repairs that can be the test. Loving the friend is a snap. Loving the old goat across the street is a time for truth. . .Spirit truth.

The masses will not know who God's remnant is

by speaking in tongues, healing the lame or caring for the blind. They will know when we can love the irritable, serve the sour and spend time with the rude. Kind to the kind? It takes no help from God to do that. To love the pain-in-the-neck? That takes God's love. . .within my heart. We can't do this. . .without Him within us!

The fruit of the Spirit is love. Fruit comes through naturally and smoothly. Fruit is borne due to a source of energy and strength from within. The fruit of the Source is not tongues, prophecy, eliteness or bragging rights. It is love through an earthen vessel too incapable of loving on it own.

"Beloved, let us love one another, for love is FROM GOD: and everyone who loves is born of God and knows God (I Jn. 4:7)."

We can be deceived. We can become ridiculous. Or, we can cower in fear of where this study might lead. Choose none of these. Dare to live the Spirit life. This book is only meant to challenge. Let us grow from here. We can offer a breath of fresh air to a dark world if we could be filled by the Spirit of God to the fulness of God. Go for the challenge!

CONCLUSION

This book is meant to encourage. Intended to aid and enlighten, it hopefully will reveal the Holy Spirit as a little more involved in the life of the common man. He was sent purposefully for such ordinary individuals.

There is only one Spirit. He worked with Jesus, with James and John, and will work with us. His mystery is His indwelling to bear fruit in simplicity. Only the nervous system of man intensifies the activity of this spiritual Guide to the point of disorder, fear and misunderstanding.

The Father, Son and Holy Spirit are one. Jesus prayed of Their oneness. It is man who spends time trying to separate the three in order to explain by earthly sense. It never makes any. The three are gloriously united. It is we who try to part the company of these for the benefit of our comprehension.

It must be concluded that the same prayer of John 17 eventually tossed us into the Holy Salad. If we could all be one; the Spirit in the carnal-formed son and in the carnal-formed citizen, the world would believe. The spreading of Bibles is not the conclusive display of Christian compassion. The walking in oneness — Father, Son, Spirit and disciples — is the grand and ultimate communication.

This material, I feel is necessary. There is a tremendous movement of the Spirit of God upon the face of this earth. Book after book concerning this subject is in print. I couldn't grip the reality of His working. It wasn't that all of the books were inferior. I am. Lord willing, this content will serve to inch those who stand upon the same ground as I toward a clearer focus of the Spirit.

Jesus set the pace. He never mis-stepped. He was as common as a Missouri farmer. He was as good as a New England fisherman. Yet, he was only a man. . .until. When he linked with the Spirit of the Father the greatest revolution started. The revolution continues to advance. This volunteer man received power.

May the human intrusion upon this topic be shattered. May we be able to discern according to spirit elevation. The Holy Spirit makes sense; Heavenly sense. His very nature baffles sights set upon the visible. "Now we have received, not the spirit of the world, but the Spirit who is from God, that we might know the things freely given to us by God, which things we also speak, not in words taught by human wisdom, but in those taught by the Spirit, combining spiritual thoughts with spiritual words."

"BUT A NATURAL MAN DOES NOT ACCEPT THE THINGS OF THE SPIRIT OF GOD; for they are foolishness to him, and he cannot understand them, because they are spiritually appraised (I Cor. 2:12-14)."

The Holy Spirit makes no earthly sense. He makes Heavenly sense!!

This material will possibly leave us with many questions. Good. It will conclude with Spirit aspects unanswered. Fine. There are areas not addressed. Great. Don't be afraid, my friend, to wonder, to think; even to be mistaken.

It is of stern conviction that the misunderstanding of the Holy Spirit is not due to His fogginess nor vagueness. Rather, it has come

114

about because of a subtle and yet profound misconception of the ordinary conventional standard of the Son of Man.

God is to be glorified in that He not only watched His only begotten die; but that He gave him up to become reduced to the classification of "person-third class."

"Who has believed our message? And to whom has the arm of the Lord been revealed? For He grew up before Him like a tender shoot, and like a root out of parched ground; He has no stately form or majesty that we should look upon Him, nor appearance that we should be attracted to Him."

"He was despised and forsaken of men, a man of sorrows, and acquainted with grief; and like one from whom men hide their face, He was despised and we did not esteem Him (Isa. 53:1-3)."

Clark Kent? Not even Robert Redford.

Finally, let it be markedly noted that it is the Holy Spirit who brings light upon Jesus. A church is to be founded upon Christ. If one is built upon the Spirit, it is mistaken. The body is the church of Christ; not the church of the Holy Spirit.

The Spirit descended to give disciples the energy to testify as to the Christ. . .not to the Spirit.

We are called — not to give witness to the Spirit — but by the power of the Spirit to proclaim throughout all darkness the excellencies of Him who brought us into marvelous light via one earthly enough to suffer capital punishment - execution upon the cross.

May we be as committed to telling neighbors about Jesus in the future; as we have been to telling ourselves that the Spirit didn't work within us in the past.